K . C .   L Y K E

LIVE
the
CHANGE!
MOVING BEYOND CIRCUMSTANCES
To Live Your Best Life

LIVE THE CHANGE!
Moving Beyond Circumstances to Live Your Best Life

ISBN: 978-1-943342-42-6

K.C. Lyke
Lyke Your Image, LLC
P.O. Box 43485
Chicago, Illinois 60643
www.Lykeyourimage.com

Printed in the United States of America
Destined To Publish | 773-783-2981
www.destinedtopublish.com

Contents

Dedication

This book is dedicated to the two most important men in my life, who are now with God in heaven.

To my dad, Richard J. Gray, thank you for being the epitome of what a real man is. Thank you for the values and principles that you instilled in me. Thank you for ensuring that I view myself as being more than a pretty face. Thank you for always putting us first, and for being my first "boyfriend," as you loved to call it. You taught me how I should be treated as a lady and gave me an awesome view of how a man provides for his family, loves his wife, and takes care of his children.

To my beloved husband, Maurice Lyke, Jr., thank you, my King, for showing me incredible love and giving me a place to call home within your heart. Thank you for being the best friend a wife could ever want or have. You will always be my forever love. I will cherish the love we share forever, upholding the legacy of your memory.

Acknowledgments

There are many who have touched my life in a positive and meaningful way. For those who were there from the beginning of my journey, thank you for your undying love and support: Richard J. Gray, Lynetta Evans-Wims, Juanita A. Franklin, and Helen White.

I would like to say thank you to my two daughters. Thank you for being the best daughters a mom could ever want. Everything that I aspire to do is with you both in mind. I want you to know that you can accomplish just about anything if you only believe!

Thank you to every teacher, counselor, mentor, and friend who was supportive and touched my life in a special way. Teachers are and will always remain heroes in my life. There are too many teachers who have touched my life to name them all. I want to say thank you to those who educated me during my time at Adam Clayton Powell Jr. Elementary, Hyde Park Career Academy, Fisk University, DePaul University, Pivot Point Academy Evanston, and Denmark Barber College.

Thank you to those who started off as friends and have become close like family: LaTonya N. Capers, Eugenia Hutchinson,

Kier Marshall, Earl Robert Lattimore III, Tamera Woods, Jimmy Fells, Rebecca Fells, Raymond Kennard, Darlene Kennard, Christy Minger, Robert Passage, Gerald Jones, Sylvia Peacock, Jennifer Evans, Nikole Childress, and my extra blessing in life, Ruth Debone-Southhall.

I would like to say a special thank you to Brian C. Stevenson. Thank you, Brian, for helping me to get out of feeling "stuck" to complete the chapter on loss and grief. I could not have completed this beautiful work without you.

Thank you to the staff of Destined to Publish! To my writing coaches, Deborah Anthony and Kara May, you are awesome. Thank you, Deborah, as your input was always relevant and on point. Thank you, Kara, you are an amazing soul, and I thank you so much for coaching me to the finish line. Marilyn Alexander, you are a bright ray of sunshine who always brought joy to my day when I was trying to reach the finish line. I look forward to working with you all on the next book!

If I have missed your name, please charge it to my head and not to my heart. Each of you has been and will continue to be a treasure in my heart. I am incredibly grateful to have known you all.

Part I

Chapter 1
My Beginning

When I was born, my teenage mother had just celebrated her 17th birthday. My biological father was 28 years old, married, and had an eight-year-old daughter with his wife. I think in some ways, my mother thought he would leave his wife and daughter to come and become a family with us. Of course, that never happened. Growing up, I was constantly reminded of how much I looked like him and how much she could have done with her life if she did not have me.

When I was about two years old, my biological mother met and later married the man I call Dad. They went on to have three children together. Throughout this book, when I use the word "Dad," I am referring to my dad who raised me.

Dad came from a close-knit family and was solid in his principles of family. My biological mother, however, was dedicated to herself, and anything that came in the way of her personal goals was surely up for elimination in her life (after she received all personal benefits from things to be eliminated). Anything happy and joyous in our lives was usually Dad's idea. He ensured that we all had what we needed and most of what we wanted. They were an odd couple in their life principles, to say the least. Dad was by far the only true parent in my life.

By the time I was about eight years old, I realized that my biological father wanted nothing to do with me. If he could not visit on his terms, he did not come around. I established my own rules and decided that Dad was all I needed; I no longer accepted calls from my biological father nor agreed to visit with him. This was the one thing that my biological mother supported me in. Why I had her support in this matter, I still do not know to this day. I am sure there is some hidden motive that benefited her.

As for my biological mother, I realized at a young age that I was not a child who would be loved and cherished. I knew I would never have a close bond of love and adoration with her. I was the burden and reminder of things lost that she could not use me to obtain (swaying my biological father to come be a family with us).

My biological mother often referenced how we dressed, how much we had, and all the material things that surrounded us as an example of her love and devotion. She did things for show, and her favorite words often included "look at my daughter, I am a great mother." Often, I was a verbal punching bag. It was extremely difficult to feel safe to share things, simply because I did not have a safe space to share my feelings. Anything I shared almost always resulted in an attack or a lecture, or it would be devalued to the point where I wished I never talked at all. This next story is the reason I chose to never share anything of value in my life again. This incident was the pivotal moment when I learned how to transition.

One day while we were driving down Lake Shore Drive, Michael Jackson's song "Man in the Mirror" was playing on the radio. My biological mother and I were the only two in the car. She turned the music down and began her familiar and frequent tangent about how much she could have accomplished in her life if she never had me. I sat there and gathered my thoughts as she kept spewing her hateful words while she was driving. I then turned to her and blurted out loud, "I did not lay down, open up my legs, and have myself." She instantly slapped me across my face. It was worth it for me to say what was on my mind, and it was quite a while before she said that statement to me again.

I was 13 at the time of that incident, and I was beyond fed up with her outbursts about me "ruining her life." I was so tired of hearing her blame me for her bad decisions. I refused to accept the idea that I was the cause of her bad life choices. I was not there when the decisions were made; I was simply one of the products of her life choices.

Years ago, we were referred to as a bastard child if we were born out of wedlock. My biological father's mother always made the comment that she knew the children her daughter had were her grandchildren, but she was not certain of any others. Everywhere I turned, there was a cold reception and a constant reminder that I never really "belonged anywhere." I never really felt "wanted" by those who were supposed to provide love and protection.

When you are born to parents who are incapable of giving you the love, comfort, and support that you need, it makes it extremely difficult to know how to function in a healthy relationship with another. Growing up, I watched those around me very carefully. I learned the type of woman I did not want to be by watching my biological mother.

I learned that I could create a life that I would be proud to live, despite how I came into the world and how I was treated.

My biological mother did things out of what was convenient for her. If she did not see a way something would benefit her, she had nothing to do with it. I quickly learned not to ask, expect, or desire love from her. As a young girl, I knew that she was incapable of healthy love and lacked the tools to be whatever it was a mother was supposed to be.

Thank God the circumstances we are born into do not dictate the outcome of our lives. I am grateful there was a greater plan for me than the one life tried to hand to me.

I share this to give you a glimpse into my beginnings, and how I can suggest ways for you to live beyond circumstance. We cannot control the circumstances we are born into, but we can control our own choices. Will you choose to live a life that you are proud to live? Will you choose to live beyond the circumstances of your life and allow yourself to focus on your goals and dreams?

I am so grateful that God had a different plan for my life that was beyond the circumstances of my life. Along my journey, there were key individuals who came into my life and made a long-lasting impact. I was honored to have teachers, mentors, friends, and sometimes strangers accompany me along my journey. They provided comfort, motivation, and encouragement along the way.

Some may call me resilient; others may say God had His hands on my life. Whatever you think as you read the pages ahead, there is one key thing I want you to know. Many can have opinions on what they think you should do and how you should feel, but it is your journey.

Only you know the true depth and impact of your life experiences. I will only share in part, hoping the things I share from my own story can help to accomplish my overall goal of this book.

I do not want you to be stuck in the pain of my story. I want you to take the pieces I share, along with the tools I share, and create your own ways to overcome challenges you may have in your own life.

As you read these pages, I want you to have a pen or highlighter nearby. I want you to mark in this book. Take notes and be involved in your reading process. Although this is not a journal, I would like for you to show ownership of your experience by writing your thoughts along the way. I intentionally left some space on pages where I really want you to do so. I do not want this book to be about pain. My goal is to acknowledge the pains of life, deal with it, heal from it, and move forward.

Let us take a journey together, you and I. I will provide insight on how to reveal areas of brokenness, heal those areas, and create your own pathway to joy. Live a life beyond circumstance and create a life you love to live. Let us live the change that we desire to have in our lives.

Thank you for allowing me to walk along with you!

-K.C. Lyke

Chapter 2

The Foundation of You

We are all unique individuals, created with things that make each of us special in our individuality. Much of what makes us who we are is established in the foundational years of our childhood. Some studies show that children learn the most in the first one to three years of life. Although tough times can occur during any point of childhood, most major emotional and physical transitions in childhood occur in the teenage years. Much of our learning during those developmental years and beyond is shaped within the structure of the family unit.

Each of us is born into a family unit. Some families are blended through marriage, some are created in adoptive homes, some are biological, and some are extended family such as close friends. No matter how your family is structured, it is important to understand the dynamic of how a family unit creates a lasting impact on who we are as individuals. I dare to say that some spend their entire lives trying to overcome issues of their childhood and things that occurred within their family unit.

Live the Change!

Just as the structures of family units are different, the dynamics within those structures can be very different as well. Some come from families that are supportive, caring, motivating, and encouraging. They have fond memories growing up and continue those healthy relationships as adults. Then there are those who come from families of extreme dysfunction, neglect, abuse, etc. Some find that they repeat the patterns of the dysfunction they grew up with, some break free and create their own path, and some stick around hoping things will change so they can receive the love and support they have always hoped for.

My biological mother was a young teen who lacked the tools to parent or to provide support and guidance. Our relationship as mother and daughter was dysfunctional, to say the least. By the time I was a preteen, I was completely emotionally detached from my birth mother. At the age of 13, I began to develop my own ideas of what a mother was, and I closely watched the interaction of other mothers and daughters who appeared to have healthy relationships. If they were people I knew personally, I asked lots of questions about their relationship and how they felt about their bond as mother and daughter. I began to develop my own ideas of motherhood and the type of healthy relationship I wanted to have with my future children, especially if they would be daughters.

I wanted to be able to give my daughters a better mother than what I had. I was determined to enjoy my life, accomplish some goals, and get married before I had children. As an adult, I now have two daughters of my own. I love my girls and support them in developing their own gifts and talents. I am always interested in the things they are naturally drawn to, as those are the areas I encourage them to develop. My children were born to a mother who was educated, married, and established in her career. My children were born to a mother who wants to love them and put their needs before my own. I created a new model of motherhood that was different from the one I grew up with.

Because of the severe dysfunction with my biological mother, it was a tug-of-war decision for me to decide to have children of my own. My husband said to me, "Honey, look at your life: you are nothing like her. You don't have to be afraid of making her mistakes. You are your own woman." Those words of reassurance helped me to decided to pursue expanding our family with my husband by having children.

I fall into the category of one who breaks free to create my own path. I am a totally different type of woman and mother from the example I was born into as a child. The first step to changing the outcome of my future as a mom was making a decision and establishing a guide on what I wanted my future self to look like. Although I was clear on the type of mother I did not want to be, I was sure to focus my energy on the type of mother I desired to become. I sought out healthy examples I could glean from. I also allowed myself to believe that I could be a different type of mother from what I experienced as a child.

Are there some things in your life that send you through a tug of war in decision making? Are they linked to childhood pains? You may have an experience similar to the one I've shared here, or you may have a different experience on the opposite end of the spectrum.

To recap, here are some of the examples of family dynamics I listed earlier:

1. A family unit that is caring, motivating, and encouraging
2. A family unit that is full of dysfunction, neglect, or abuse (physically and/or emotionally)

Live the Change!

Some find themselves repeating the patterns of their dysfunction, some break free creating their own path, and some stick around hoping change will occur and they will receive the love that they desire.

- As we revisit these examples of family dynamics, which category do you see in your childhood family unit?

_____

_____

_____

_____

- Now take a moment to reflect on your family unit growing up. Are there things that were great?

_____

_____

_____

_____

- Do you find yourself implementing those "good" traditions into your life?

_____

_____

_____

_____

_____

- Are there things that were not so great?

_____

_____

_____

_____

- Do you still find yourself implementing those "not so good" things into your life?

_____

_____

_____

_____

- Why? Why do you implement the "not so good" things into your life?

_____

_____

_____

_____

Please do not just skip ahead to the next paragraph.
I want you to place the bookmark on this page and
really give it some thought.
Really answer the questions.

I will be right here waiting for you, once you have done so.

This is how we do the work.

This is how we live the change!

Now that we have taken some time to reflect,
I want to tell you something extremely important:

You are not broken!
You, my friend, are powerful beyond measure!

The truth is, when you are a child, the adults in your life have the power to make all of the decisions. The children are forced to live the consequences of those decisions, whether the decisions are good or bad. When you are connected to a family unit, it is like a small country. The parents are the leaders who make all of the rules, decisions, purchases, connections, negotiations, etc. Those who live under the rule of the parents are bound by those decisions until they become of age and/or are able to move out from under the rule of the parents and establish a life of their own. Sometimes, depending upon cultural dynamics, adulthood does not terminate the rule of the parents.

Why am I going into all of this? Oftentimes, many grow up and become their own person, but never resolve the issues of their childhood. Some may not have the opportunity to confront the rules they grew up under. Some parents are not open to dialogue or are not capable of using the words "I am sorry" if hurt or pain was caused. You may now be a parent with children of your own, as you are reading the words on this page. Recognizing and understanding the family structure you were reared in can be very beneficial during your tenure as a parent.

Now as an adult, you have the power to make the decisions. It is so important to take the time to reflect on, acknowledge, and work through the issues of your childhood. Remember the questions I asked in the section prior? Let's delve into the "why."

We all find ourselves repeating some behaviors or habits we learned in the family unit that we grew up in. The key is whether you are implementing the good or the not-so-good things you learned from your parents. If we do not work through and acknowledge the "why," we can find ourselves repeating things we experienced from our childhood that we really do not want to repeat.

Remember, you are powerful beyond measure! Now let us establish some new habits to filter into our own families that we have already created or will create someday (if you so choose). Family is what you make of it, and you do not have to have children within your family structure to be a family unit.

Let us explore some healthy habits for a family structure. Do you want to eat dinner together and share your day? (I did this with my dog when I was single.) Do you want to celebrate or not celebrate certain days? You create the rules now.

Sometimes we repeat things we were taught without knowing why we continue to do things a certain way. As I share a personal example, I want you to think of some things you would like to change or implement in your family structure.

Many years ago, I was homebound due to a work injury. I endured eight months on crutches and had a lot of time to think and reflect in this new state of being. Using crutches for eight months forced me to slow down and reevaluate just about everything in my life. One day, I decided to watch a movie I purchased but never made time to watch. As I began watching the movie, I immediately started to admire the actor's naturally curly hair. I paused on every scene where her hair was styled differently and drooled over her hairstyles. At the end of the movie, I went to the bathroom mirror and began to imagine what my hair would look like if I allowed my natural curls to grow in. I then began a dialogue with myself and asked myself some questions:

"I love curly hair, so why do I wear my hair straight again?"

"I wear my hair straight because my mother started straightening my hair when I was a small child. My mother hated my curls because she found my hair difficult to manage."

"I hate wearing my hair straight! It is so flat, limp, and has no body when it's straight."

"I LOOOOOVE volume and curls!"

"That is it! I am going to grow my natural hair. I will embrace my curls."

Once I made the decision to embrace my natural curls, I immediately threw out all of my straightening products and tools. Over the next couple of months, I allowed my hair to grow, and I cut all of the straightened hair off of my head. During that dialogue, I also realized how much I loved hair, so I decided to become a licensed cosmetologist. I have happily embraced my curls for almost two decades. Now that I embrace my curls and love my hair, I am able to pass that positive self-image on to my daughters. They both love their curly hair as well.

(Note: Just in case you are wondering, the movie that sparked my natural hair decision is *Pride* starring Terrence Howard and Bernie Mac. The actor with the amazing hair in that movie is Kimberly Elise.)

This is an example of how we can repeat something we have learned without understanding why. We can continue to execute an action on autopilot without questioning why we are following the path we were placed on by another. When we evaluate our actions and make conscious decisions about our actions, we begin to move in true purpose. That defining moment not only allowed me to reconnect with my natural hair, it also led me to my current career path.

If we make decisions and do not look at the "why" behind them, we run the risk of repeating the not-so-good things, and we may be baffled when we have that "I sound just like (or am acting just like) my father/mother/caregiver" moment. Also, allowing yourself to ask "Why?" can lead you down a groundbreaking path in your life, like it did for me in the moment that I shared above.

Always remember that if you experienced dysfunction as a child, it is no fault of your own. If you are now an adult, you have the power to write your own story and choose how you want to live your life despite how you grew up. It is okay and sometimes necessary to allow yourself to question things in your life. Be sure that you are truly happy with the path you are on. If you do not find joy, begin to ask yourself some questions. Asking questions could be the beginning of a breakthrough.

If you find that you have suffered severe trauma and would

like to work with a licensed professional, there is no shame in seeking professional counsel to obtain the healing you deserve. Please be sure to talk to a medical professional for referrals. I will talk more in the next chapter about seeking professional counsel if needed

If you are reading this section and you feel like you had a great experience growing up and love everything about your childhood, that is fantastic! Reflect on those great experiences and see if there are some areas you would like to expand on and make even better.

As much as I would love to fix all things, I know that I cannot, nor is it my place to be a fixer of all things. My hope is that at the end of this journey, I will have provided some tools, encouragement, and guidance for you to begin the process of making changes in your life that you feel are necessary to change.

Sometimes while we coast through life on autopilot, it can take a jolt of divine intervention for us to realize that there are some things that we *need* to change. In the next chapter, I will talk about how to recognize cues that could indicate that you are headed towards change. Let us explore how to work with the inevitable instead of fighting against it.

Chapter 3
Bridging the Past to Your Present

*I*n the introduction, I shared a small part of my background growing up. I did not have the love and support of my biological mother. Along my journey, I received most of what I needed from a collection of mothers.

For the first two decades of my life, I did what I call "collecting mothers." Any woman who was sincere, positive, kind, loving, and took a genuine interest in my life became a part of my collection of mothers. I have learned something significant from each one of them. If they had their own daughters, I watched how they interacted with them and many times had an opportunity to speak with them.

I am still in contact with some of them as I type these pages. Some of these relationships have lasted at least 20 years. Often I place the word "Momma" before their first name, placing honor and value on what they have contributed to my life. All of these women are the true definition of the African proverb "it takes a village to raise a child."

Thank you to my collection of mothers who believed in me and taught me how to embrace who I am. Thank you for the countless hugs you gave when needed and for offering your shoulders to cry on. Thank you for being voices of reason and providing sound counsel. Thank you for those who are prayer warriors and cover me continuously. Thank you for aiding in a transition from the pain of not having a mother I could receive such things from, into having an experience of true motherly love.

Pain can often serve as an indication that change must occur. Pain usually indicates an area in the body that has suffered from some form of trauma, injury, or hurt. Healing can only occur once pain has been evaluated and addressed.

I am often asked, "What is it inside of you that keeps you standing, despite all that you have been through?" Some can take the philosophical route and talk about resilience and all of the childhood studies spanning decades. Some can take the spiritual approach and say, "It was truly the hand of God on my life." I will try to answer as best I can from my own perspective. I think I can best do that by way of a story:

When I was in college, I was taught by some of the most brilliant minds at Fisk University. In particular, I had a political science teacher who was also an attorney. We would receive some of the most gut-wrenching and thought-provoking assignments in the form of 10-20 page essay papers.

One semester, I took this instructor's philosophy class along with another class by the same instructor. The most memorable assignment I had in that philosophy class was this question: "Are leaders born, or are they made?" We had to choose a side, and in true attorney fashion, we had to argue our point in a 20-page essay paper.

It was one of the most difficult assignments I had ever completed. I was truly in the middle, believing both elements can be possible: leaders can be born, and leaders can be made. Ultimately, though, I could only choose one side, and I decided that leaders are born. In this document, I referenced some of the greatest leaders in African American history – we were at an HBCU, so why not use all black leaders? I was in my creative genius as I poured both facts and educational opinions into the document.

In this assignment, I could not help but think of all the things I had overcome in my own life. There are those who experienced far worse things than me. There are those who had all the support, love, and money there is in life but still ended up living lives of drug or alcohol addiction. Why had I not gone down those paths of destruction? Was this something I was taught, or was it something I was born with?

This is my conclusion. The core of who we are, we are born with. Some are born with artistic genius, athletic superiority, ease at absorbing and understanding languages, musical talent, and the list goes on. They have an inherent gift they are born with. Of course practice, cultivation, and coaching can make their gift more superior, but they were just born with "it." In contrast, if you try to teach someone something and there is no skill to build upon, it does not matter if they are taught by the best in the subject field, it will not make them great.

Now back to my answer to the question: I have no idea why I was not consumed by my circumstances. There was always a feeling that I had to do better. I had to find a way to put myself through college and create a better path. No one had to teach me that. That was inside of me for as long as I can remember. I had cousins in gangs, was born to a teenage mother, suffered sexual abuse as a child, and had all odds stacked against me. But there was a fighting spirit on the inside that pushed me. I knew I did not want to be like the environment I grew up in. I was born with that determination and belief that I wanted more.

Along the way, I met teachers, mentors, friends, and strangers who believed in me. They helped to cultivate what was already inside of me. I always had a belief that I could do better even when I did not know how. If I chose to have children someday, I wanted to be better for them. Even as a child, my driving force was always my future children and wanting to be the best person I could be.

So I fall on the side of believing that I was born with the belief that I could, and that belief came from God. That is what has kept me from crumbling; God is the reason that I stand. My maternal grandmother used to say, "On Jesus the Solid Rock I stand; all other ground is sinking sand." I had a determination to move beyond what I could currently see in my life. The belief that I could do more and have more in my life has helped me to move forward even with all odds stacked against me. I had a strong praying grandmother with unshakable faith, and I know that part of who I am comes from her.

I was once asked, "If you could change anything about your life, what would you change?" I did not hesitate when I answered: "I would change absolutely nothing. The things I have gone through and the experiences I have endured are what has molded and shaped me into the person that I am today." That was my response almost 20 years ago, and I stand by that response to this day.

My life experiences are reference points. I can look back on situations, circumstances, and experiences and think, "My God, I made it through that." When I think of the things I have been through, I know I can handle what lies ahead. I learned early in life how to shift and embrace transitions. This is the key to shifting my past to a transitional bridge into my present and future.

Chapter 4
Recognizing When You Are in a Transition

Transitions in life come in many different forms. Oftentimes, a life transition is accompanied by growing pains, feeling uncomfortable, frustration, and at times trauma. These feelings and experiences of emotional changes are an indication that change is inevitable. Recognizing when you are in a transition can help make the process a bit more bearable. It is also an opportunity to put support systems into place, surround yourself with positive people, and have access to tools to help navigate a major life change.

It is important to recognize when you are in a transition to help balance the emotions and changes that come along with these challenges of life. It is better to feel that you have the tools to weather a storm versus feeling blindsided or as though you are in a whirlwind of uncontrollable currents tearing through your life.

A transition is a necessary bridge for you to cross over into the next phase of your life. Sometimes the "next phase" is celebrated and welcomed, and sometimes it can be painful and dreaded. Transitions of life can be an undercurrent that can take you under if blindsided, or if the undercurrent sweeps you into an abyss of multiple major life transitions all at one time.

Some transitions are embraced, like a job promotion, college graduation, increase in pay, or making a new friend or associate. Then there are other transitions that are not embraced and could bring emotions of dread or resentment, like death, divorce, demotion, and other losses. Sometimes fear can arise in transitions that others may consider positive or good, like marriage, relocation, or adding a new family member (through births or adoption). As with all things, the effects of a situation on an individual depend on each person's temperament, experiences, perspective, and self-perception.

One of the keys to recognizing that you are in a transition is to identify if a major change has occurred or will soon occur in your life. Changes can bring newness, which can also bring a level of stress or frustration, even if the change is a "good" change in your life.

I like to describe transitions as a bridge between the old and new (moving from a current situation to a new situation). When a change is occurring in our life, there is movement from one state of being into the new state where the change lies. The transition is the bridge. I created these diagrams as examples.

The example below shows a person who starts as a single individual, enters into a romantic relationship, and then moves into marriage.

Transition (the relationship is the bridge)

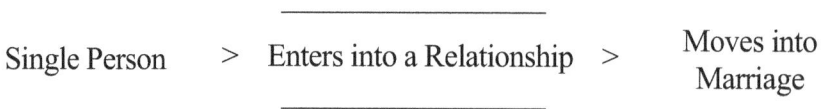

Single Person   >   Enters into a Relationship   >   Moves into Marriage

In this example, there is a single person who is living their life, making decisions solely for themself. Once the individual meets a person they are interested in sharing their life with, they enter into a committed relationship. The relationship is the transition. During this time, two individuals are getting to know each other, determining which direction their lives are headed in as a couple, etc. Once the relationship is established and the decision is made to enter into marriage, the current situation of the relationship quickly becomes the bridge of transition.

The transition is unique to each individual experience and can be loaded with multiple mixed emotions like happiness, stress, excitement, fear, and bliss, to name a few. Marriage is just one example; for another, let's look at a common transition of death and grief. Every person will experience death and grief at some point in their lives. Both death and grief are natural parts of life, and they are also some of the most difficult and gut-wrenching transitions in life.

In this example, one can start off their day with everyone they love alive and well. At some point in the day, a phone call is received with devastating news that a beloved person has passed away.

Transition
(Loss of a loved one)

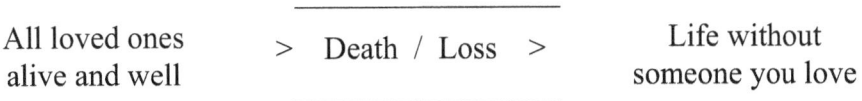

All loved ones alive and well	> Death / Loss >	Life without someone you love

You can apply this simple flow chart to any situation if you are unsure and would like to determine if you are in a major life transition. There are different levels of transitions. Some are minor, while others are major, causing a noticeable shift in your life. Major transitions are more impactful and can sometimes cause a transitional phase to last a lot longer than we would like it to.

Another common feeling in a major life transition is feeling like the bottom just fell out of your life. You may feel out of balance or out of control of your circumstances. You could also feel like you have no control in your life as a whole.

- Have you ever found yourself in a major life transition and did not realize it until you had processed through it?

_____

_____

_____

_____

_____

_____

- Would it have been helpful to identify the transition in the beginning?

_____

_____

_____

_____

_____

_____

• Take some time to think about your current life situation. Are you in a major life transition now?

_____

_____

_____

_____

_____

_____

• Multiple life transitions can occur at the same time. In this section, what did you discover to help you in your current transitions?

_____

_____

_____

_____

_____

_____

Please do not just skip ahead to the next paragraph.
I want you to place the bookmark on this page and
really give it some thought.
Really answer the questions.

I will be right here waiting for you, once you have done so.

This is how we do the work.

This is how we live the change!

Now that we have laid the foundation for recognizing when you are in a major life transition, let us explore some things you can do to make that transition more bearable and manageable.

When you are in a major life transition, it is very important to sort out your tasks and to-do list into things that *must* be completed and things that you would *like to* complete. This is an important key to setting priorities and managing overwhelm. Things that *must* be completed are non-negotiable and have to be accomplished. Things you would *like to* complete are flex items and can be accomplished at a time that is not so immediate.

It is so important to be gentle with yourself, accept that you are human, and accept that there are not enough hours in a day to complete every single task that you think is necessary. This will help you to set realistic goals and turn down the pressure of overwhelming feelings.

With small adjustments or deletions to your schedule,
you can create a balance in your overall life
that eliminates overwhelm.

Example: You may have a deadline to complete a report at work, and you would also like to get home to cook dinner. A solution could be to complete the report and order delivery for the night. Both tasks are accomplished with modification. You get the report completed, but you will not be able to cook dinner, so a compromise is to order something for delivery.

You can use this basic chart below to separate the critical things from the not-so-critical things that can be modified or adjusted, as in the example above.

Things I have to complete	Things I would like to complete

Remember the example above: the report from work is something you have to complete, and dinner is a "like to complete" task that was modified to take-out delivery. Dinner does not have to be a home-cooked meal. There are no severe consequences from ordering take-out, but there may be a consequence from not completing a crucial report with a hard deadline.

The idea is to lighten the feeling of overwhelm. Always remember there is a choice in every situation. The choice before you may not be ideal, but there is a choice, and you have the power to choose.

Let's break down a decision into percentages. I want you to realize that 80% of what you have to overcome is your thoughts and perception of your circumstance. The other 20% is the action you must take in order to change your circumstance. If you get stuck in your thoughts, you will never take action to change. That is a fact.

Can you think of a time when you had to accomplish a task, but you talked yourself out of it? Did you build a mountain of dread with your thoughts? Did you replay in your mind how long it would take? How awful the task would be? How you do not want to do what you need to do?

In times of transitions, decisions have to be made, like at any other time in your life. This can become more complex if we allow negative thoughts to drive our decisions. Am I saying to ignore your feelings? Absolutely not. I am saying do not allow yourself to live in your feelings to the point that you are unable to make life decisions.

Let us revisit the example of death discussed previously. This time, I will share a bit of the most difficult story in my life.

My husband's passing continues to be the most difficult transition in my life. What made this loss so difficult was that he became my family. I felt our relationship made up for all of the hell I had endured in my childhood family. Now the only normal, loving relationship in my life was being taken away. The best way that I can explain the depth of grief is this: The greater the love, the greater the level of grief.

Every negative emotion in the dictionary, I am certain that I felt. Sometimes I still have moments where I need to process some of those feelings. The best advice I received was to allow myself to feel and to be gentle with myself.

Although the bottom had fallen out of my life, the rest of the world continued. I still had to make decisions financially. The basement flooded, and repair decisions had to be made. I had to decide if I wanted to continue the job I was working at the time. The decision had to be made about whether I would relocate, as we were in the midst of making those plans as a couple. So many decisions needed to be made.

I took a lot of time off from work and allowed myself to grieve. I took care of the most important bills and was okay with letting whatever was not immediately important fall through the cracks. I was managing the best I could in the midst of what felt like a fight for my own life. No one had to tell me that my life would never be the same. The horror of the loss was a reminder of this massive life transition.

Death of a close loved one is an ongoing transition. Although time helps to ease the grip of grief, it does not completely eliminate the sting of the loss. After my husband passed, I attended counseling for two years. I allowed myself to seek help because the magnitude of the loss was beyond what I wanted to handle and felt I could handle on my own. I will talk about this more in the chapters ahead, but seeking counsel can be a necessary step when dealing with major loss.

Losses in life bring a level of disappointment and hurt. In the next section, we will address the disappointment that comes with loss.

Dealing With Disappointment and Loss

Life is a roller coaster that we all must ride. Along that journey, there will be disappointment and losses along the way. Although loss is a natural part of life, it can also be one of the most difficult parts of life to accept. Loss is a taking away of someone or something we desire to continue to have in our lives. Loss can fall into two categories: things that happen in our lives beyond our control and things that happen as a result of decisions we make in our lives.

Sometimes we are disappointed with decisions that we make, and other times we feel the effects of decisions that were made by others in our life. There are also things beyond our control like natural disasters, unexpected death of a loved one, or being laid off from a job. When one is disappointed, it is because there is an emotional tie or investment in a certain situation, event, or decision. The disappointment comes when there is a certain level of expectation that is not met.

Although we have little to no control over some things in life, we can place ourselves in a position to receive the support needed to cope with such losses. Some of those things include seeking counsel, surrounding yourself with supportive, loving people and allowing yourself to grieve your losses.

A loss can be temporary or permanent. Sometimes you can manage a temporary loss better than a permanent loss. Sometimes you can go through a stretch of life where it is smooth sailing. In those times, all is well, life is good, and there may be a feeling of euphoria. Then there are other times when the storm of life comes, and it could feel like you are drowning in loss or traumas. It is quite possible to experience multiple traumas and not feel as though you have time to recover before the next tsunami of loss hits.

Regardless of the type of loss you are experiencing, it is

important to understand that dealing with loss is not optional. Loss is a crucial part of your emotional journey that must be addressed and dealt with. Trying to avoid and run from the effects of loss is like trying to run from your own shadow. When you stop running, you will realize that the weight of the loss has been running alongside you. Once you take a moment to stop running, all of the emotions, feelings, and anguish will unpack themselves and cause you to deal with them during the most inopportune time in your life.

Addressing grief and loss is like peeling the layers of an onion: there are many layers that will cause you to tear up, get choked up, and feel as though you are ready to stop digging through them. Remember that you must breathe through the process, take breaks when needed, and keep pulling back the layers to completion. This is not an easy or simplistic task. This will involve moments of vulnerability, commitment to the process of your healing, and allowing yourself to be free to explore your feelings and emotions.

Now I will begin to explore this delicate process of closure and healing in such a difficult and multilayered area of life. Below are some topics I will attempt to cover and make useful no matter where you may land in the spectrum of loss.

There is no road map to help navigate grief, we all have our individual experiences. What I can share is that the depth of your grief is anchored to the depth of your love for an individual. The greater the level of love, the greater the grief experienced once that love has departed.

When death occurs and the one who passes away is not close to your heart, you can send a card and then, within a few days or weeks, forget that the person has passed. When someone close to your life dies, however, the sting is unbearable, the pain is permanent, and the longing is lasting. Grief is not a light switch that can be easily turned off or on. Grief is a process that you must allow yourself to feel and navigate through.

Oftentimes, grief is explained in terms of stages of loss. I believe that explaining grief in this manner can give the perception that once you experience a stage, it is now completed and over. Grief is more like a series of tidal waves, moving much like an ongoing roller coaster ride. These rides can be filled with multiple peaks, valleys, and surprise drops that leave your stomach in your throat. Just as you think the wave has passed, another comes to take its place.

If you have ever experienced a loss close to your heart, you are sure to understand the description above. In dealing with close losses, know that it is an ongoing process. There are some days that are better than others. Some days, it feels as if your loved one just passed, even if the death occurred years ago. Then there are times when you may feel that you can survive the loss and are okay to move forward. The tidal wave can come when you least expect it. It is often triggered by a life event like a wedding, graduation, birth of a child, or other significant event where the sting reminds you that your loved one will not be present. It is perfectly normal to experience moments of sadness in these times when you feel you should be "over" the loss by now.

Once you have an understanding of how grief can present itself, it is important to acknowledge the disappointment and emotions brought on by the loss. This may sound basic, but sometimes we can be so busy trying to "get through" the loss that we do not allow ourselves to feel the loss and be okay with the emotions it is causing us to experience. This is an important step in the healing process.

I mentioned earlier that grief could appear in many different forms. Let us take a moment to acknowledge some areas in your life where you may have experienced some level of loss but may not have acknowledged those losses. This is important to also see challenges you have overcome as well, and to know that you can meet new challenges that will arise in the future.

Below are some examples of types of losses. Feel free to take a look at the examples below and then fill in the blank chart to acknowledge some losses in your own personal life.

Examples

Life Event	Loss	Change as a Result of Loss
Friendship	Grow apart	Loss of friendship
Job promotion	Layoff	Loss of income
Pregnancy	Miscarriage	Depression
Marriage	Divorce or death of spouse	Loss of finances, home, cars, custody of children; widow/ widower
Health	Loss of limb, sight, ability to walk, etc.	Will to live

Your Personal Losses

Life Event	Loss	Change as a Result of Loss

Please do not just skip ahead to the next paragraph.
I want you to place the bookmark on this page and
really give it some thought.
Really answer the questions.

I will be right here waiting for you, once you have done so.

This is how we do the work.

This is how we live the change!

Always remember that it is an important step to allow yourself to go through the process and not allow others to put a time limit on your grief. Your emotional journey is a very personal one, and it is not another person's place to dictate to you how long that should last, how you should feel, and when you should "get over it." Comments like that come from insensitive people who generally have not experienced a loss that is extremely close to their heart.

Although those around us can have the best intent, their approach can sometimes cause more harm than help. If you recognize that someone around you is not being helpful in their approach, try to communicate your needs and let them know how their lack of sensitivity affects you. Sometimes, it may be necessary to separate yourself from individuals as you feel you must. It is a delicate line to walk: you want to make sure you are not too isolated, as that can lead to further grief and depression in some cases.

Having healthy relationships and healthy boundaries is crucial in times of loss and disappointment. It is crucial to be able to effectively communicate your needs and set boundaries during times of loss, grief, and disappointment.

During times when I experienced unimaginable loss, I had a few individuals ask me many question about loss and how to deal with it. One question that stands out in particular is "What do you think is the hardest part of loss after the death of a loved one?" The answer may vary for each individual, but I believe the hardest part is the days and weeks after the funeral is over.

During the time that you are planning and making arrangements, most people want to feel useful, chip in, and offer a helping hand. However, after the funeral is over, that is when everyone else goes back to their "normal lives." In that moment, you are left feeling the impact of your loss and knowing that your life will never be the same. This time can be the most isolating and lonely after the loss of a loved one. It is really important to communicate your needs while maintaining healthy boundaries.

This is when the series of tidal waves of grief will begin to take effect. Each individual is different, and that will determine which emotion will surface. Some start with denial, anger, or just feeling numb and not showing any emotion initially. Remember, there is no correct way to grieve a loss. It is important to allow yourself to feel and to be surrounded by those who are loving and supportive of your needs. It is possible to experience the same level of grief even if you have not experienced the death of a loved one. Ending a friendship, terminating a long-term relationship, or relocating to a new city and leaving your friends and family behind can cause strong emotional grief as well.

How long one may grieve is also an individual experience. Each person is different, and it is important to be kind to yourself and not place an unreasonable timetable on yourself to "complete grieving." The good news is that there is life on the other side of grief. The key to living that life after losing someone or something important is to find something worth fighting for and deciding to fight. This will serve as a new anchor in your life.

Having something worth fighting for comes down to having a purpose: a reason to get out of bed, a reason to set new goals, a reason to choose to be happy. These are some examples of small accomplishments that become huge accomplishments when picking up the pieces after a major loss.

If you are someone who has yet to experience a major loss in your life, this section can help you to support others in your life who may have experienced such a loss. This can also serve as a future reference, as life is sure to bring seasons of change. As I stated before, death is a natural part of life. As we live, we will also experience death at some point in our lives. There are also losses that can be just as traumatic as death; loss of health, mobility, sight, finances, and housing are just a few.

For those who have yet to lose a close relative, what I can offer is this:

Cherish those you love.
Always communicate love
and express your feelings of appreciation.
Tell those in your life that you love them, and tell them daily.
Tell those in your life how much you appreciate them and why.

These are simple and basic, but if you make it a practice to do these things often, it is less likely that you will wonder if those you love know how you feel about them. When the day comes when the one you love is no longer here, you will never have the regret of not expressing your feelings and love towards them. There is a peace in knowing that you said everything that needed to be said.

We have spent some time talking about loss due to death and other unforeseeable life changes. There are also consequences and losses that can occur due to decisions we make in life. Each decision comes with consequences, whether they are good consequences or bad ones.

Have you ever had an extreme level of excitement that came crashing down and was shattered by disappointment? I think it is safe to say that we have all experienced this on some level. This leads to asking how can we avoid or lessen the effects of such emotions when disappointment pays us an unexpected visit. The first thing I will say is to always go into your situations knowing that disappointment and loss is a possibility. You do not dwell on the possibility, but know that it can occur.

Let me give you an example. If you talk to any newly engaged couple, I am certain someone has taken it upon themself to tell them about all the negative pitfalls of marriage. Someone always has a story of a nasty divorce, custody battle, loss of property, and/or loss of finances in a divorce. Is that a possibility for this couple? Yes, it is possible. But in the midst of their happy moment, that is the last thing they would like to hear about.

My approach is a little different. You can decide to live your life in fear and never take a chance at anything, or you can decide to make the best choices in the situations you are given. In making such decisions, know that a not-so-favorable outcome could occur, but a great outcome can also occur.

There is much to be said about making good decisions for your life. Sometimes you can find yourself in the position of having to make a quick decision. There are other times when you can take more time to make the best decision possible. If you have time to make a decision, use that extra time to your advantage. Avoid making a rushed decision if it is not necessary. Sometimes taking the extra time to think a situation through, and to heed that feeling in the pit of your stomach that this may not be the best choice, can save you a lot of heartache and grief that comes along with a not-so-great decision.

One of the best decisions I ever made was to chronicle all the losses I have ever experienced in my life. Writing them all down and acknowledging each loss, the difficulty of each loss, and the growth that came as a result of each one was a very important step in my healing and respecting my own journey.

As I type these pages, I must share that it was a very difficult and daunting task to capture the importance of what I want you to take away as a reader in this section. I feel that I best explain my process by sharing a personal story. This sharing is more layered as I attempt to share the difficulty and complexity of this subject.

My first memory of loss was the death of my baby brother who lived a few short moments after being born prematurely. What made this loss so difficult is that my parents rarely talked about, acknowledged, or even mentioned his existence beyond the first few months after his death. I held a baby brother in my arms, and then we left the hospital without my baby brother. This laid the foundation for loss in my life. I had no guidance on how to deal with the loss or how to process and grieve such a loss. A few months after my brother died at birth, I was hit with another loss. This loss was my innocence being taken away by molestation at the hands of an older cousin.

As the years moved on, I experienced more losses. I mourned the loss of my grandmother, which was by far the most traumatic and gut-wrenching loss of my childhood. The years continued with multiple losses of grandparents, aunts, uncles, and the list goes on. I had a high school sweetheart commit suicide and found myself facing yet another loss. By the time I hit my twenties, I had experienced enough loss to last a lifetime. This did not exempt me from future losses. I then was hit with the tsunami of losing my husband, the love of my life, to a heart attack. In picking up the pieces, I suffered two miscarriages trying to conceive the babies my husband and I planned to have via in vitro fertilization. I lost my spiritual father to cancer, my dad who raised me died after a long battle with diabetes, and I know more losses lie ahead, as that is a natural part of life.

I can look back on all of these losses and see the gems of strength, love, perseverance, and fortitude that were planted in my soul along the way. Looking back, I know that I can face anything that lies ahead because of the things I have lived through in my past. Often times, change is looked upon as a dirty word. Change is met with resistance and often disappointment. I want you to know that as painful as change can be at times, it is a necessary element to help you evolve in your life journey.

Regardless of what has happened in your life, what has happened to you, or what has happened around you, I want you to know that you have the power to live the change in your decisions. You can choose to be more than your pain. You can choose to work along with change to be your best self.

Living the change does not mean that you do not feel or acknowledge your past. It means that you take all that has molded and shaped you, and you move forward through the pain until you reach the other side of it. This is a continual journey throughout life. You will often face change, losses, and pain. Work through them, even if you have to carry them a bit until you process out of the pain and are free to live beyond the pain.

I am sure that this section has opened some wounds for some. The next section will provide guidance on how to deal with some of those opened wounds that may now be exposed. Let's talk about seeking counsel when needed.

Seeking Counsel When Needed

Seeking counsel is a sign of strength: knowing when to ask for help.

I am a strong advocate of seeking counsel when necessary. If your situation feels like it is beyond your ability to manage, please seek professional counsel. You can start by discussing the way you are feeling with a medical doctor. I have used professional counseling services in the past and will continue to do so whenever I feel that it is needed.

A counselor is much like a medical partner that one can use to help navigate difficult periods in life. There is absolutely no shame in seeking a medical partner to assist during tough times such as death, divorce, or any other major life transition. This is a stance I had to grow into, as it was not the culture of my immediate family. I was not taught to seek outside help or counsel. Growing up, it was drilled into me that you did not talk about family issues that happened inside the house to those outside of the home. There were times when I broke that rule, as there were things I really needed to talk about. I had my teachers, friends, and mentors that I truly trusted and could talk to during the challenging teen years.

The real breakthrough came while attending Fisk University. One day while in a psychology class, we were talking about family dynamics. A comment that I made led the instructor to talk to me after class. It was such a defining moment in my life. She is a licensed psychologist, and she offered for me to come off campus to her office, where she counseled me for several weeks and maybe even months at no cost.

That was some of the most valuable time in my life. I was able to unload the years of carrying secrets and things I was told as a child that I could not talk to others about. It helped me to heal from and let go of the shortcomings of my biological mother. I did not just graduate with a college degree, I graduated as a whole, healed, and complete person.

I am a strong advocate of seeking professional counsel. In my case, it was my instructor in college. God Almighty put this angel instructor in my path. She was sensitive to my sharing and took the extra time to talk to me. She offered her professional skill as a service, and I am forever grateful to her. The time I spent in her office gave me the strength to draw a line in the sand and never look back.

Finding a good therapist is similar to finding a good mate. Not all mental health professionals are the same. The process of finding someone to fit your needs can be challenging and rewarding at the same time. Let us first start by explaining the difference between a psychologist and a psychiatrist. The most basic way to know the difference is that a psychiatrist has the ability to prescribe medication.

As I said before, there is no shame in seeking counsel. I just want to be sure to take the time for those who may never have considered this option and give you some insight to make the best decision for your life. If a psychiatrist is recommended, I suggest knowing what your recommended treatment plan includes, such as which medications are suggested, the side effects of those meds, and how long it is suggested to use them. This gives a clear outline of a treatment plan and sets an expectation of when you can wean off the meds so they are only needed short term to reduce dependency. What I can say, as with any medication, is to be sure you follow the orders of your medical professional and do not try to take yourself off meds, as this can cause more harm than you may anticipate. Knowing when to start and stop meds helps to reduce dependency and helps you know that there is an end to that form of treatment.

If you are dealing with severe depression, substance abuse, or alcohol, a psychiatrist may be recommended. If you are exploring seeking professional assistance with trauma, loss, and other life issues, you may seek a psychologist. A psychologist can always refer you to a psychiatrist (who can prescribe medication) if needed or if a more severe mental health issue is suspected and diagnosed.

For those who are not comfortable with the traditional counselor, you can consider the alternative of seeking a Life Coach. There are times as a Certified Life Coach where I have worked with a client who was also attending therapy with a licensed psychologist. Oftentimes with a medical professional, you are given a treatment plan and then sent home to execute that plan on your own.

As a Life Coach, I am here to help clients after they come home and need to implement changes. Sometimes knowing what to do is not enough. In some cases, it is necessary to have a professional in place to help make such drastic changes to ensure success while at home. My job as a Life Coach is not to prescribe a treatment plan but to support someone as they carry out a prescribed plan by a licensed medical professional. I welcome people to have all tools to navigate through personal difficulties. Although there are many things I can coach a client through, there are times when a medical professional is encouraged and recommended for my clients to seek.

My job as a coach is very similar to how I am talking to you right now in this book. It is not my job to tell you what to do, as you have a brilliant mind and most times know what you should do. My job as a Life Coach is to help you overcome obstacles that keep you feeling stuck. My job is to help you navigate pitfalls and to accomplish the things you already know you should do. I provide support for those who may lack a support system, and I help you to come to your own conclusion and act upon your decisions with confidence.

If you take a look at some of the greatest coaches of all time, they do not give athletes their abilities or skills. The coach's job is to help the athlete expand on the skills they have in order to become greater at their craft. A coach can see the blind spots and weaknesses. A coach can love you beyond the now because they have a glimpse at the greatness of your future. That is what I have to offer as a Life Coach. Life Coaching is an alternative for those who may not feel as comfortable in beginning with traditional therapy.

Whatever avenues you choose when considering seeking counsel, please choose what is comfortable and best for you as an individual. Please do not attempt to tackle tough transitions of life on your own, especially if everything on the inside of you is screaming for help. Asking for help is not a sign of weakness. Asking for help is a position of power that will allow you to heal and move into the next level of your greatness.

As we prepare to move into part two of this book, I hope that you take some time to reflect on your life journey. There is so much to appreciate about who you are and how far you have come.

Recognizing When You Are in a Transition

Part II

I want you to take a few moments to reflect on some of the topics we have covered so far. We have delved into some pretty heavy topics. I hope that you have taken the time to reflect on some things in your own life. Reflection is a way to see where you have come from, be grateful for your growth so far, and know that you have the power to face the next steps ahead.

The next part of this book is dedicated to laying a foundation for taking the next steps and some ways you can do just that. The upsets and pains experienced in life are merely life transitions. If you can quickly realize when you are in a transition, you can gain better control of your expectations and emotions as you cycle through the transitions. This will help you to live the changes in your life.

In the chapters ahead, I will give you some specific things you can focus on during life transitions to help you shift any situation and your perspective on it.

This is how we do the work.
This is how we live the change!

Chapter 5
Put Your Own Mask On First

One of the best examples to describe self-care is when a flight attendant tells you to put your own mask on first during an emergency evacuation. This is such a powerful illustration and example of how important it is to tend to your own needs prior to providing care to another individual, including small children. As a caregiver, it is very easy to develop a habit of putting the needs of others before your own. It is almost a sense of duty you feel to place the needs of those you love before your own needs.

If you pay close attention to the flight attendant, the instructions are to secure your own mask before you attempt to secure the mask of someone traveling with you (which includes a small child or an infant). As a parent or caregiver, those instructions seem absolutely unimaginable. If there is a need for oxygen and we are told to provide it to ourselves and then to one we care for, we are used to doing the reverse: providing for and meeting the needs of those we care for and then ourselves (if we provide care for ourselves at all).

We all know that oxygen is essential to breathing and breathing is necessary to continue living. If thought is really given to the instructions, one can realize it really is the best approach in an emergency situation. How could you possibly attend to the need of another if you pass out due to lack of oxygen while trying to meet that person's need? Although this is suggested during emergency situations, I dare to say this should also be applied to everyday life situations as well.

When I gave birth to my second daughter, I was extremely exhausted tending to a new baby, breastfeeding, while also trying to spend time with my toddler, maintain a house, and tend to every daily need in our family. Tired and fatigued, I would skip meals trying to fit it all in. There were times I did not have time to shower, comb my hair, or do anything necessary for myself. I attended sessions with a therapist who specialized in women's heath, and she reminded me that I was no good to my children or anyone else if I did not take care of myself. She reminded me that self-care is not selfish but necessary to be the best version of myself for my family and for myself. I had to begin putting my own mask on first before I could tend to the needs of my family.

Have you ever experienced a time in your life where you felt breathless, or had difficulty breathing due to overwhelm or fatigue? Often, the solution is to cut back on the number of activities, stay well hydrated, and get plenty of rest. Does that sound familiar? It is usually what your doctor will tell you if you are fighting a bad cold or the flu. This is a great practice to incorporate daily.

I often tell my daughters I have to sit down and eat to rebuild my strength. I will tell them, "If Mommy falls out, I am unable to do anything for you. I have to sit down and eat or take a moment to recover."

Live the Change!

I am learning that it is essential for me to eat before I serve dinner. It is necessary to get myself dressed and ready for the day before I attempt to get my daughters dressed for school. When I would do things for my family first, I noticed I always ran out of time for myself. There was always something I did not do for myself before I would leave the house to start my day. If I took care of my needs first, I always managed to meet the needs of my family even if there seemed to be "no time."

Taking care of yourself first is not selfish, it is necessary! When you are the best version of yourself, you are able to provide the best for yourself and for those you love. Let's do a little experiment. Question: Do you always put the needs of others before your own? If yes, continue with the assignment; if no, read it anyway.

If you are a parent or caregiver, I want you to get up 30 minutes before your family awakes. For example, if everyone in your household wakes at 8:00 a.m., I want you to wake up at 7:30 and take those 30 minutes to drink a cup of coffee, tea, hot chocolate, water, juice, or whatever your morning beverage of choice is. Be sure to take a shower, get dressed, etc. These 30 minutes are all about you.

After you take care of your own personal needs, then wake your family and proceed with your morning tasks. Please do not do anything for anyone until you take some time to "put your own mask on first." This is the much-needed oxygen to get you through your day.

I want you to continue this for three days. Notice how you feel, your mood, how you interact with those you are serving, if you appear to have a bit more patience. Whatever differences you notice in yourself, I want you to write them down. If you are currently doing these things in the morning for yourself, share this assignment with someone in your life who could benefit from putting themself first.

I would love for you to fully commit to yourself so you don't feel anger, frustration, or irritation for not taking time for you. In the middle of tending to your own needs, I want you to resist the temptation to stop to start dinner, laundry, packing lunches, etc., and really take that time for you. It's best to take time to rest and recover to avoid burnout.

Believe me when I tell you that I have experienced this firsthand. After I gave birth to my second child, I burned both ends of my energy level. Being a widowed mom, I was on my own with a newborn and a toddler. I was breastfeeding, and that is a land of sleep deprivation all by itself. Add in trying to maintain the house, prepare meals, complete laundry, keep groceries in the house, and the list goes on. When I discovered I was dealing with the worst case of postpartum depression there is, I immediately sought out the help of a women's health therapist. It was this kind professional who reminded me that I needed to take time to rest and recover. All of the household things could wait and they would definitely not see completion if I ended up in the hospital.

This was a reminder that I needed to return to the very principles that I live by and teach as a Life Coach. I had to allow the dishes to pile up a day or two and choose sleep and a shower in the 15 minutes I had before my baby was screaming for milk or my toddler needed another meal. I had to let some things go in order to provide basic needs for myself.

Sometimes making time for oneself is easier said than done. Some really struggle with finding time for self-care. In the next section, I will talk about self-care and how to achieve it.

Self-Care: What Is It, and How Do We Achieve It?

Self-care is not selfish;
it is necessary to be the best version of myself.

In the previous section, I gave you an example of self-care – putting your own mask on first – and how we can take time to determine if we are making time to care for ourselves. Self-care is so important that I have an entire program in my coaching business dedicated to this topic. Now I want to take some time to delve into self-care. During this season of life, we may hear a lot about self-care. Self-care is being talked about in the media and online. You may ask yourself, "What exactly is self-care, and how do I achieve it?"

I want to take a moment to speak directly to the ladies. Sometimes as women, we feel the need to do all things, and it is easy to fall into a pattern of putting yourself last or not making time for yourself at all. Everything becomes more important than taking care of your own basic needs. What I will say to you is that you matter, your needs matter, and if you are not making time to really show yourself that you are important, it is absolutely necessary that you start right now!

To the men, I will say that it is an innate trait of men to protect and provide and sometimes not make time to check in with yourself emotionally. Where women can neglect themselves physically, I find that men do the same thing emotionally, and sometimes both men and women neglect themselves in both areas. Men, it is okay to emotionally check in with yourself and allow yourself to feel. It is important to acknowledge those feelings more often and not push them down and to the side.

Many may find themselves responsible for taking care of other family members, extended family, and/or children. In the hustle and bustle of life, it is easy to forget to take care of yourself.

When you take care of yourself, you are providing
the best version of yourself for you and those who are around you.

Here are some suggestions to begin to build a healthy self-care routine:

Get a great night of sleep

Most studies say that you need an average of seven to eight hours of sleep each night. My suggestion is to get the amount of sleep that is best for your lifestyle. Some feel their best with six hours of sleep, while others may need nine hours. Listen to your body and adjust your sleep schedule to that which fits your needs best.

Sleep is usually an issue for most clients I speak with. There is just not enough of it in our lives. What I will suggest is to set a bedtime. I know it may sound a bit basic, but if you set a bedtime and prepare to wind down in preparation for sleep, it helps your body get into a relaxation routine.

For example, if the goal is to be in bed by 10:00 p.m., you want to start winding down around 9:00 p.m. Turn off bright lights and use a small table lamp to "dial down" your environment in preparation to rest. Use that 30 minutes prior to bedtime to execute your bedtime routine (shower, wash your face, brush your teeth, etc.).

Another suggestion I will make is to have a clean environment to sleep in. Remove papers, work, computers, and phones out of your resting environment. The bedroom should be a place of relaxation. It is important to make sure your bedroom communicates relaxation and does not motivate you to continuously work when it is time to rest.

These are basic things, but they are quite challenging for most to implement. Rest is essential to recover and restore the energy used throughout the day. These basic things will make a significant difference in how well you rest at night and how much sleep you are able to get.

Have a "dump list"

Sometimes it is hard to fall asleep at night if you are one who thinks about everything you have to do the next day or in the days ahead. Writing down those things to free your mind to rest is very helpful. I call it a "dump list." It is a way to free your mind from thoughts or tasks you can write down for the next day.

Also, you can use this technique to write down the most important tasks you would like to accomplish the next day. Remember, prioritizing your tasks helps relieve the feeling of overwhelm. Chose the three to five most important things you need to accomplish the next day and write them down.

Eat a healthy, well-balanced meal for maximum energy

I am sure you have heard it many times how important a well-balanced diet is for your health. I want you to think about food as fuel for your body. If you look at a motor vehicle, you know it is impossible for it to operate without the correct fuel amount and type. There are different types, but we know that the most efficient fuel allows a vehicle to operate at peak performance. The food that you put into your body is the same way. You can choose to eat anything that you desire; however, if you want your body to operate at peak performance, you must give your body healthy, nutritious meals for maximum energy.

Drink plenty of water to stay well hydrated

The human body is about 70% water. As you burn energy, your body releases moisture through sweat and perspiration. It is extremely important to drink water to replenish the amount of water our body loses through perspiration throughout the day. Sometimes you can mistake dehydration for hunger. Staying well hydrated can help some from overeating during meal times.

Add body movement throughout your day

My clients know that I do not like to use the word "exercise." It comes with so many negative associations for some, especially if they have struggled with weight issues at some point in their lives. I like to use the term "body movement." As human beings, our bodies were made to be in motion. A body in motion is a healthy body! Here are some examples of things you may naturally do that put your body into motions and can serve as a way to "work out": gardening and yard work, walking, running, dancing, and sexual activity (yes, I said it!).

Have healthy relationships in your life

I think it is safe to say that if you are alive and breathing, you are in some form of relationship with another human being. Whether it is a friendship, family relationship, romantic, work relation, and so on, we are all in some type of relationship with other people. It is extremely important to have healthy relationships in your life. Some relationships we are unable to choose, like family and coworkers. Although we cannot choose the people we are related to and work with, we can choose to have healthy boundaries in place in those relationships. Being able to effectively communicate your needs, expectations, and desires in relationships helps to establish healthy boundaries.

Another key component to healthy relationships is making sure those you are connected to and surrounded by are positive people. Those you spend the most time around have a great impact on your mood, energy, and drive. It is important to reduce the amount of negativity in relationships to continue the health of the relationship.

Have fun!

As adults, it is so easy for us to be engulfed in work, responsibility, and serious tasks that it can cause us to lose that ability to access pure fun and joy in our lives. Be sure to add laughter throughout your day. Watch a comedy, play jokes on your friends or loved ones, and allow yourself to have good, clean, old-fashioned fun.

I want you to take some time to think of how you relax or reward yourself that does not include food, alcohol, or anything that could be considered an addictive source. Revisit the section that walks you through how to reward yourself with something other than food. Some like to use cooking and baking as a form of relaxation and that is okay. If you like to bake, I suggest you give treats away as gifts to those you love. The idea is to think of some things you like to do and incorporate them into your week.

If you like to bake, set aside some time in the week to bake a new treat. Or if you like to read, buy a new book and read a few chapters during wind-down time before bed. I want you to schedule self-care time like any other appointment in your life. Taking time to care for your self is essential to your mental and emotional health. Mastering this skill will help you to be more balanced and happy in your life.

At this point, you may think there are a lot of activities or assignments in this book. The idea is to pace yourself and interact with yourself throughout this process. Revisit the section above and list areas you need to improve and areas where you do well in regards to your own personal self-care.

Manage your self-care

Areas to improve	Areas where I do well

Making time to care for yourself is a crucial life skill to master. It will make you a much happier person and so will having work life balance. Work life balance is essential to continuing this journey of self-care.

This is how we do the work.

This is how we live the change!

Work-Life Balance

You may wonder why I have a section dedicated to work-life balance. In pursuing a more balanced and meaningful life, we must assess the very thing that takes the majority of our time, and that is "work." It is important to ensure that our work is meaningful and provides a sense of fulfillment for our life desire, and it is also important to balance time spent working with allowing time for other things in life outside of work. This can be a challenging area for some to achieve. The demands of careers, jobs, work responsibilities, meetings, reports, etc., can often overshadow family time or remove you from the very thing you are working for, and that is your family or a sense of fulfillment in life.

I have met some who have never taken a vacation, or who "go on vacation" with their family only to work during the entire "vacation." It is so important to balance your family and work life. My hope is for everyone reading this page to know how precious time is and that you should maximize your time with the ones you love. We all have a set amount of time on this earth. Let us all remember that our time is precious and limited and be sure to take time to enjoy the things we are working for.

Of course, we have to work to provide for and take care of our loved ones and ourselves. We also owe it to ourselves to take vacations. It is crucial to take time to relax, renew, and restore our minds and bodies. Taking a vacation and establishing a relaxation and rest routine looks very different for each individual. For some, taking a vacation could mean taking a couple of days to visit a particular destination. For others, taking a vacation could mean staying still and enjoying the comforts of home.

However you decide to vacation, be sure to unplug from the

work phone, watch a funny movie, snuggle up with your dog, cat, or loved one, and catch up with those you love. Connection is often more important than destination. Give some undivided attention with a "no phone" policy in place. Talk, play an old-school board game, really connect with each other, and enjoy quality time.

Try to really connect with whatever you are doing without worrying or thinking about work. Catch a game of golf, take a stroll outside, look up and take in the sights of the environment around you. Some of the best ideas and thoughts come when you take time to free and clear your mind.

Sometimes I am asked, "How do you accomplish the things you do?" My answer is simple: when I take my last breaths, I want to have absolutely no regrets. I live my life on purpose. I want well-balanced and healthy relationships with my children, and I want to explore this beautiful world we live in. I do all of that by having work-life balance. When you take time to unplug, you sharpen your ability to return refreshed and better able to focus and tackle the tasks waiting for you.

As a person who is very task oriented, it is important for me to have people in my life who remind me to have fun and balance my need to accomplish tasks. My husband was the person who reminded me to put my work down, do something fun, and do it often. This was a great reminder and provided great balance to my life. Now in his absence, our oldest daughter is the person to remind me that I am working too much. She will often say, "Mommy, can we have a dance party? You promised we can this week." She keeps me balanced, and it is a wonderful reminder to take the time to enjoy the beautiful gift of motherhood.

There are other times when taking time away from work will

lead to the thought of, "There has to be more to life than this." Clearing the clutter of your mind will allow you to ponder on your "why" in life.

Are you happy with the work that you do?
Take some time to access your current career.

Things I love	Things I want to change	Things I need to change

Remember that we spend the majority of our time working. I believe that this is something worth taking the time to assess and evaluate. Take a try and see how you feel after this exercise. This may lead you to the belief that there is something greater in life than where you are right now.

Please do not just skip ahead to the next paragraph. I want you to place the bookmark on this page and really give it some thought. Really answer the questions.

I will be right here waiting for you, once you have done so.

This is how we do the work.

This is how we live the change!

As you find ways to have work life-balance, it will ultimately allow you to connect with a greater level of joy. Connecting with your joy is an important step to living the change.

Connecting with Your Joy

Have you given thought to what brings you pure joy? Maybe mentioning the word "joy" at the end of the last section caused you to begin to ponder on what really brings you joy in life. Joy is a feeling of great pleasure and happiness. Have you given thought to what brings you that feeling?

A lot of times we get caught up in the grind of life and forget to engage in things that bring us joy. Many years ago, I had a mentor tell me to stay connected to the things that brought me joy (dancing, music, artistic creations). At the time, I did not understand why he was providing such advice. As I matured and became a wife, a mom, and a business owner, I came to understand exactly why he gave me this advice.

Oftentimes, we lose our joy in the midst of living life. While climbing the career ladder, taking care of loved ones, or advancing our education, we find ourselves on the treadmill of chasing goals and dreams. It is easy to lose your joy in the midst of the chasings.

If we are not careful, we can find ourselves in situations where we are upset with our spouse, children, parents, coworkers, and every other person in our lives. The frustration builds from a place where we have neglected to provide a fundamental basic in life: joy. Those around us can add to our joy, but it is not their responsibility to make us happy. As individuals, we are responsible for our own joy.

Do you know how to turn on your happy switch? Do you know how to make yourself happy without another person? When I ask this question, I often receive the "deer in headlights" glare.

As adults, we are so conditioned to think about all the things we "have to do" that we are often totally disconnected from the things that bring us joy. Also, many struggle to answer questions similar to those below. Take a look and see if this is difficult for you as well.

- What brings you joy?

_____

_____

_____

_____

_____

_____

_____

_____

- How do you keep more of that in your life?

_____

_____

_____

_____

_____

_____

_____

_____

In American culture , most celebrations involve food. Whether it is a wedding, birthday, baby shower, or job promotion, there is food and possibly alcohol nearby. It is really important for you to establish a healthy way of celebrating that does not add to your waistline. How do you allow yourself to experience pleasure that does not involve food, alcohol, cigarettes, or any other substance you may ingest?

Please take some time to make a list of at least 10 things you can do that bring you joy.

Joy List

Activity	How often do you do this activity?

Just in case this is a true struggle for some, I will list some things one may consider as a reward or treat for yourself. Remember, it can be small or big. I will stay small to midrange:

A massage	Gardening
A good movie	Drawing or painting
A vacation	Singing
A shopping spree	Dancing
Helping others	Playing music or an instrument
Hot bubble bath	Building or creating something

- Does it put you in a happy frame of mind to think about the things that bring you joy?

_____

_____

_____

_____

_____

_____

_____

- Can you find a way to incorporate those things throughout your days, weeks, and moments in life?

_____

_____

_____

_____

_____

_____

_____

Please do not just skip ahead to the next paragraph.
I want you to place the bookmark on this page and
really give it some thought.
Really answer the questions.

I will be right here waiting for you, once you have done so.

This is how we do the work.

This is how we live the change!

If you take a look at a weekly schedule, I want you to find a way to schedule some of your joyful activities throughout your week. Look at the list you made above and begin to schedule joyful activities at least once a month. After you decide which joy activity you will accomplish each week, please be sure to store your activities in your personal calendar. Treat this like any other important appointment that should not be canceled unless it is an emergency.

Look at the example weekly schedule below and choose a date and time for your joy activity for each day of the week:

Sun	Mon	Tue	Wed	Thurs	Fri	Sat

It is so important to know how to access your joy. Remember the previous section where I talked about personal responsibility? Being personally responsible for your own joy means that you can access and spark joy whenever you want or need to.

If you love to cook new meals, can you try a new side dish or dessert once a month? If you love to dance, turn on the music and dance it out in your living room. Can you commit to taking a dance break once a day for 10 minutes? The idea is to show you how you can make time for things that are fun and bring balance and joy into your everyday life.

One of the common complaints I hear from mothers is that they no longer have time for themselves. There is just not enough time to do the things they love to do. As a mom with two small children, I know exactly how that can feel. What I decided to do is to incorporate my children into the things I love to do.

Here are some family favorites. Arts & crafts projects: each month, I ask my girls what they would like to make for a project. I check to make sure we have supplies at home, and we have a coloring party once a week. We make cards for upcoming birthdays, make magnets, or I give them colors, paper, and foam and let them be creative. Another favorite is dance parties every week: we turn on the music, grab some instruments, and dance it out. It is a great cardio workout and stress reliever for me, and my girls have a blast. Cooking is very therapeutic for me, and I love cooking for my family. I let my girls help mix whatever I am making, and I place all things in the oven for them. They like helping and getting their hands dirty.

Below is our weekly joy schedule. I give myself the flexibility to change days and times around, but I do not cancel or remove our joy activity out of our family week

Sun	Mon	Tue	Wed	Thurs	Fri	Sat
Cooking and Baking	Pamper Day (self-care)		Dance party after work/ school			Arts & crafts projects

We can use our children as a reason why we cannot do something, or we can use them as the motivation for why we should do something in our lives. One thing that my favorite aunt told me is "Your kids won't stay little, they will grow up, and this phase will pass." This was a reminder for me to embrace these times while they are little. It is challenging at times, but adding some of the activities above reminds me to enjoy my children and share my passion and love of art, music, cooking, and dancing with them.

If you are not a parent, you can still apply the same principles above. Remember that you have to make time for yourself. It is so easy to lose sight of your joy as you focus on providing for and being there for others. As much as it is important to have that balance of family and fun, it is equally important to make time for yourself.

If I were to tell you that you only had one week to live, how would you spend your time?

• What negative people would you eliminate from your life?

_____

_____

_____

_____

_____

• What vacation would you plan?

_____

_____

_____

_____

_____

• What fancy restaurant would you seek to make reservations at?

_____

_____

_____

_____

_____

• What new thing would you purchase for yourself?

_____

_____

_____

_____

_____

Please do not just skip ahead to the next paragraph.
I want you to place the bookmark on this page and
really give it some thought.
Really answer the questions.

I will be right here waiting for you, once you have done so.

This is how we do the work.

This is how we live the change!

I want to challenge you to live your life on purpose. Live every week like it is your last week on earth, and be sure to place some joy throughout your week. Be it small or big, be sure to schedule time for yourself. I schedule pamper days on Mondays. Mondays are the days I schedule a massage, choose a new nail polish color, or buy a fresh bouquet of flowers. I make a conscious effort to do something nice for myself.

There are times when it is absolutely necessary to have "me time." This is time that is solely dedicated to yourself. Although it may be challenging, it is important to set aside time for yourself. It is extremely important to take care of yourself even if you feel that your time should go to your family or other obligations.

As we connect with our joy, it often leads to another necessary connection. I call this connecting to that which is greater. There is always a greater purpose beyond ourselves. When we allow ourselves to explore this principle of life, we allow ourselves to connect to more fulfillments in life. Let us explore how finding that "why" allows you to have a sense of completion within yourself. Live the change!

Connect to That Which Is Greater

Regardless of your spiritual beliefs, I believe that we all end up at the crossroads of life, wondering if there is more to life than what we are currently experiencing. Often this is caused by longing and wanting more out of life. Have you ever had the feeling like there has to be more to your life – that there has to be more than working a job, paying bills, raising kids, getting married, and maybe squeezing in some fun along the way?

I started this thought journey in my early twenties. I had a burning feeling that I was supposed to do something meaningful but did not know exactly what that something was and how I was supposed to achieve it.

What I always believed is that there is something greater than myself. I believe that this has always kept me grounded. I always knew that whatever I ended up doing had to have purpose and meaning. It is of extreme importance that I am able to look at myself in the mirror and be happy with my decisions.

Even in times of frustration and seeking to know the "why" in a season of my life, I know there is a greater purpose than what I may see. I talked to you earlier about using gratitude as a tool to combat sadness. What I can also tell you is that finding a greater purpose in life outside of myself is the greatest goal in my life. I strongly believe that things happen for a reason and all things have a specific purpose in life.

Have you ever experienced something and thought to yourself, "I have no idea why I had to go through that, it was an awful experience"? Now with that same experience, some time will go by (maybe months or years), and you look back on that experience and say, "I still do not like that I experienced that situation, but I now see how much I have grown, learned, or can use from that experience." I can honestly say that this has happened with just about everything I have experienced in my life. At some point, I look back and see the connection a particular situation had in my overall development and growth.

When I was a young girl, I did not always have the best example of what a healthy family unit was. I knew on the inside that I wanted more, and I wanted to be a better example for my children than the examples I had before me. It was that inner knowing that was the driving force for me to overcome and believe I could be more. Wanting better for your life does not mean that you belittle anyone else. It simply means that you have personal goals you would like to achieve for yourself, and there is nothing wrong with that.

It is a greater knowing and belief that will keep you going when all things around you will make you want to stop and give up. Stay the course! That is what my beloved Independent Sales Director Nikole Childress would say. Do not give up, and keep going!

Connecting to something greater than myself saved my life and gave me purpose, hope, and a future to look forward to. This connection also gave me the courage to travel an uncharted path in my life and seek out others to help me find the tools to be a more healed and complete person. That is how I lived the change I desire in my life.

This section is not meant to be a how-to but rather a reminder. Remember to look up to the sky, look out into the environment, connect to the knowledge that there is something greater beyond yourself, and be committed to exploring what that means for you as an individual. Explore how you will choose to connect to that greatness beyond yourself. How can you serve others? How can you bring joy into the life of another? How can you move beyond your own life and make an intentional effort to connect to something greater than yourself?

I know that the force on the inside of me is a gift. For whatever reason I was chosen to have that gift to sustain me, I am grateful. I realize that not everyone has the ability to reach inward, and some reach outward to other vices that can lead down a road of more pain and possible destruction. If you share the gift of being able to reach within to serve as your own source of motivation and encouragement, please continue to do so. If reaching inward is a challenge for you, be sure to reach for positive influences that will enrich and enhance your journey to that which is greater than yourself. As we reach forward, we do so with a knowing that there is a process to life. Let us explore how to embrace that process along our journey.

Chapter 6
Embrace the Process

Your journey is your journey.
-Nikole Childress

Many years ago when I first moved back to Chicago after college, I worked at a university in admissions processing. My job was to take calls and answer questions from those who had applied to the university and were awaiting decisions.

This was a position that helped me to learn to embrace the process. I remember one call in particular. The student was a transfer applicant who was coming from a community college to complete the last two years to obtain a bachelor degree. The student asked why the process takes so long and if there was any way to "skip the process." I politely responded, "You cannot bypass the process; this is what is necessary to obtain admissions." As the words came out of my mouth, they instantly resonated with me as well.

Have you ever gone through a situation and wished there was a fast-forward button in life? Have you ever wished you could just skip the situation you are going through? As painful as it may be, and as senseless as it may seem, it is a part of your journey and cannot be skipped or bypassed. I believe that the most difficult situations can bring out the best in our character. If we allow ourselves to go through the process, we may discover there is something in the situation we can learn from or use to create good.

As I type these pages, I hope that there is something in my process that is helpful for you. It is not always easy, and we may not understand why we are going through something. We can always choose how we use the situation and learn from it. I choose to share, I choose to grow, and I choose to use my process to help others.

Everything in life has a process. Sometimes we can be in such a rush to get to the next phase or the next level that we do not allow ourselves to enjoy the process. I have found many lessons, friendships, and revelations during my many processes in life. Fighting the process only prolongs it and sometimes can cause us to repeat a lesson. I've found that when I embrace the process, it becomes a bit more doable.

Everything in life has an appointed time and season. If you take the time to look back over your life, I am sure you will recognize a time that was not comfortable but that you now realize was necessary. The formal dictionary definition of "process" is "a series of actions or steps taken in order to achieve a particular end." It can also be "a natural or involuntary series of changes."

As life takes you through a series of actions or steps, there are many possible lessons you could learn along the way. It is absolutely normal to allow yourself to go through stages of questioning, frustration, and even anger. At the end of all of that, I would say, "So, what is next?"

You are in the situation and it does not seem to change much. You are in a slow-moving process and would like it to end quickly. The best advice I can offer is to ask yourself a series of questions: What can I learn from this? What can I take away to apply to other areas of my life? Is there anything that this situation is trying to show me about my life or those who are a part of my life?

I find that asking questions helps to move me out of panic and frustration and into a mode of problem solving. This small shift in approach can be a game-changer in how you go through a process that may not be so pleasurable or desired. Once I change my focus, it changes my attitude, which ultimately changes my ability to discern the situation more clearly. I initially thought a situation was the most terrible thing ever, but after reassessing, I discovered that the same situation was filled with a variety of surprises and blessings along the way.

Does this apply to every situation? Absolutely not, though in most situations, I can honestly say that in time, I have found there to be more good that comes out of a process than bad. When the dust settles and the pain subsides, we can think more clearly. A perspective can change and help you realize there was so much more in the process than what meets the eye.

So, what can one possibly do to make a terrible situation more bearable? I am glad you thought to ask. One of the greatest examples I can think of for a process is how a pearl is made. An irritant, usually a parasite, is caught in the oyster, mussel, or clam. As a defense, the oyster begins to coat the irritant with nacre. Multiple layers cover the irritant for up to about three years, and in the process, a beautiful pearl is formed.

Live the Change!

Can you relate to the pearl? Can you think of a situation in your life that seemed to last for years? Did anything good come out of that irritation and frustration you endured? If you ponder long enough, I am sure you can think of something positive. Did you gain more strength, determination, courage, and endurance? Even if you think the situation was horrible, there can be a tiny bit of good if you allow yourself to acknowledge it.

As I write the pages of this book, I am undergoing a personal process. This process of writing is helping me to have a greater appreciation of my stance. Knowing that I still stand despite the currents of life that tried to blow me down, I love who I am even more. I am embracing the champion spirit that I have and appreciating myself on a deeper level. I am taking time to stand in the sun more often and see my journey as something to be grateful for. I thank God for creating me in the manner in which He has. I am grateful that I live the changes that I desire to have in my life.

Each day, I am learning to embrace and appreciate the things about me that my husband loves so much. This process continues to unlock new dimensions of who I am and allow me to appreciate my uniqueness more in depth. I am wrapping my arms of gratefulness around this process, knowing that it is adding to my coat of armor, which radiates the beauty of who I am.

The process of life can be messy and frustrating, but it does not mean that nothing beautiful can emerge from the experience. Can you list some processes you have undergone in your life? What did you learn or take away from them?

Life Processes (experiences)	Lessons Learned

How have you lived the change?

As we embrace the ups and downs that life can bring, we often share these moments with others. It is important to know the types of boundaries you would like to have in your relationships as you navigate the ups and downs of life. Healthy boundaries are a way to ensure balance and equilibrium in your everyday relationships. Can you live this change?

Healthy Boundaries Equal Healthy Relationships

Don't make someone your priority if you are only their option.
-Unknown

The above quote was spoken to me by a dear friend many years ago. At the time, I believe that we were talking about relationships and the disappointments we can sometimes experience. Her words were offered at a time when I was at a crossroads in a relationship. From that day, the words "don't make someone your priority if you are only their option" has always served as a compass for me to know if I was in a relationship that was worth continuing. My needs in a relationship are more than how a person makes me feel; it is extremely important to know how someone will show up for me and to know if I can rely on them in my time of need.

I learned at an early age what characteristics were important to me in a relationship. In the beginning, it was being able to identify what was missing and did not work. I soon took that understanding of what did not work and used it to help me discover the traits and characteristics I absolutely needed and required in all relationships.

My dad describes love as doing what you do not want to do. In relationships, we often find ourselves doing things that we may not choose to do, but opt to do out of the love and respect that we have for another individual. It is very important to make sure those you are in relationships with are willing to make sacrifices for you just as often.

There were times when I did not want to watch a football game with my dad, but I watched those games with him because it was a way to bond, it was something he enjoyed, and it was a way for us to spend that quality time together. My dad actually thought that I loved football, but I just loved spending time with him, and football was the way I could get that bond and have quality time with Dad. Now I look back on those times with fond memories.

The above was one example from my life. Take some time to think about different relationships in your own life. Are they balanced? Are you always giving in the relationship, while the other person is always taking what you have to give but never giving you the same support, love, dedication, etc.? Are you always taking what others have to offer in a relationship and never returning the same kindness and support to the other person? If you answered yes to any of these questions, it is likely that you are in an unbalanced relationship. Do you see areas where you both give to support each other's needs?

I do not want this to be an act of "taking score" but a way for you to make sure you are in a balanced relationship with others and there is a give and take on both ends. You want to make sure that you are surrounded with people who are encouraging, supportive, and willing to assist in your time of need. You also want to be sure to reciprocate the same level of love and support you receive from others.

Utilize the chart below to assess the state of your relationships.

Person you are in relationship with	Things that are balanced	Things that are imbalanced

Do you see a place for improvement or growth?
How will you live the change?

I have met individuals who had a hard time saying the word no. Some put themselves in unrealistic situations because they were unable to tell someone they are unable to do something for them. I am grateful that I do not struggle with this; however, I have worked with clients who struggle severely with finding balance in relationships. Remember that it is our own personal responsibility to bring joy into our own lives. When two joyful and happy people come together, that joy overflows within the relationship. If someone is deficient in joy, it is easy for the joyful person to feel obligated to ignite joy in the other person's life.

There is an honor in having the ability to bring joy into the lives of others; however, it should not be a burden to be in a relationship. There are times when relationships are absolutely beautiful and the hope is that it never ends. There are also times when a relationship has run its course and consideration must be given to how you can continue in a healthy manner or if it is best to dissolve the relationship altogether. This can bring about change, which is an ongoing transition in life.

Change: The Path to New Beginnings

Sometimes you have to roll with the punches and punch back!

Most people are a little resistant to change. If we are completely honest, we do not like it. Change means we have to find another way of doing something that we are used to doing. Change is necessary, however, and it is the path to new beginnings. Think of the seasonal changes in nature from fall to winter. After winter, spring transitions into summer. Each season brings about a new change. In fall, the trees begin to shed their leaves, the air becomes a bit crisper, the sunlight becomes shorter, and we know that winter is right around the corner.

Change is inevitable and something we can learn to embrace. We do not like change at times, but it is the necessary bridge to open new chapters in your life. Earlier I shared with you how I ended up on my current career path. Asking myself some thought-provoking questions while homebound with an injury for eight months gave me a lot of time to reflect. I spent weeks thinking about my life and what I could do to combine happiness with passion to provide a way of living for myself. I truly wanted to accomplish this goal. That series of questions and answers helped me to uncover my passions and unveil the things that really brought pure joy into my life.

What I can say for certain is that change can be terrifying as it connects us to the unknown. I also know that facing your fears can help you cross over into your greatest achievements. I was afraid at the thought of quitting my job, which provided a steady source of income and health benefits. I thought about how I would afford health insurance, cover the expense of my mortgage, and pay other monthly bills.

Next I thought, "What happens if I allow myself to continue on the path I am on without making any changes?" I knew that I absolutely hated my job. I hated all of the restrictions and constrictions it placed on my life both professionally and personally. I also did not like being in a profession that was not family friendly. I knew I wanted to have children someday, and continuing in the job I was in was not realistic if I wanted to be physically and emotionally available to my family.

All of these thoughts lead me to the conclusion that I had to make a change. My life, emotional wellbeing, and happiness depended on me making these necessary changes in my life. My attitude was this: "I am afraid, but I will say out loud, 'Come on, fear, come go with me to accomplish my goals and create some happiness.'" I continue this saying to this day. Now I say, "Come on, fear, come go with me to accomplish the things God will have me to do." Fear may be present initially, but eventually as you move forward, fear can and often does turn into excitement and joy.

In my moments of questioning, I made a commitment to search for the answer until I found a solution. I made a commitment to myself. I chose to place my quest for happiness above my fears. Each day, I made small efforts that accumulated into what some would consider a huge change. Always remember that big goals are an accumulation of tiny accomplishments strung together.

Now, as I look back 13 years later, I know that moment of change was such a profound crossroads in my life. Learning what my passions are and following that path truly led to my success in the beauty industry and a life of total happiness. Connecting to my passion brought me to professional connections, friendships, mentors, and business ventures.

It was this choice of change that laid the foundation for every future opportunity I have yet to uncover. Each day that I awake, I am happy with the life that I live. I am happy that both my professional and personal lives are used to add value to myself and to the lives of others. I am the best version of myself, and I continue to look for opportunities to grow and expand.

It is never easy to willingly choose a path of change. But if there is no change, there is no true growth. Embrace the change and know it brings you closer to your personal evolution. Change is the necessary ingredient of life. We do not like change when it comes, but guess what? Change will come anyway. Let us be a little proactive when we approach change. Let us view change as an ally and not an enemy.

The road to change was not always easy, but it has always been gratifying. Despite it all, I chose to live beyond circumstance and create the life I so desired to have. I chose to allow my passions to lay the path to my success… and the journey continues. I live the change – will you?

Choosing a path that is well traveled can be convenient, but it can also be very crowded. There is something to be said about having the courage to embrace that which makes us unique. If we are all unique as individuals, why should we expect our path in life to be similar to another? You are unique and unlike any other. I love that each person has their own set of fingerprints, including those who are twins. There is absolutely no one in the world quite like you! Take your prints and leave your unique mark in this life journey. Take a deep breath, embrace change, and let us explore the power of walking your own path.

Chapter 7
Walk Your Own Path

You are enough... Step into YOUR vision!
-Nikole Childress

It takes an extreme amount of courage to take the path less traveled. On my mother's side of the family, she was the first to graduate high school. No one had ever attended college in her family. It was acceptable to drop out of high school and work a job to provide for your family. It is a beautiful thing to work to provide for your family, and it is also a beautiful thing to want more than what others believe you are capable of achieving.

I was an alien in the family. I had these dreams of leaving my parents' house, attending college, and becoming a successful businesswoman someday. At that time, it was laughable to my family. Growing up, I was referred to as the bastard child on my biological father's side of the family. I was born to a young teenage mother who did not possess the tools to help me achieve the goals I wanted to achieve, nor was she interested in my goals. I was told by my parents to figure it out myself if I wanted to go to college; I was on my own because they had two other children younger than me to raise. No one in my family could guide me down a path they had never traveled before.

Although my dreams were laughable to my family, I had teachers, friends, and mentors who believed I could accomplish them. I immediately stopped telling my family what I wanted to do and only talked to those who believed in what I wanted to achieve. As I type these pages, I am a two-time college graduate, I hold multiple professional certifications, and I am an owner of two businesses. You can achieve your goals and dreams if you believe in yourself.

Sometimes it is difficult to feel belief in yourself if you are unable to share with those you love because they may be negative and doubt your dreams. Sometimes, however, it is necessary to place some degree of separation to protect your dreams. A great example is a couple that is newly pregnant. Oftentimes, the doctor wants you to make it through the first trimester, as that is when many miscarriages occur. Many choose to withhold the news of pregnancy from family and friends until the second trimester or beyond.

Your dreams and goals are just like pregnancy. Oftentimes, you can become discouraged in the beginning stages of your dreams, as you may not have all of the details of how you will accomplish the things you desire. Just like that newly pregnant couple, you have to guard your dreams like a new developing baby in your womb. There are some individuals who will doubt you, spew negativity, attempt to steal your joy, and try to sabotage you along the way. You have to be extremely careful of those with whom you share your dreams and aspirations.

The crucial advice I will give you is to hold on to your dreams and believe you can accomplish them no matter what others think. Surround yourself with those who believe in you. They can be friends, colleagues, and sometimes strangers. Focus on those who believe in you, and do not worry about the doubters. One of the most important things I did as a young adult was to stop sharing my goals with those who were negative. It is amazing how those who have not accomplished their goals can feel so strongly that you cannot achieve your dreams because they failed to achieve their own.

I am a conqueror, I am a warrior, I am the child of the Great I AM. However you speak to yourself, please be sure that it is positive. If you are incapable of positive talk, surround yourself with those who are capable until it rubs off on you and you begin to echo such sentiments. Your journey is unlike any other. Let your experiences be your prize possession like your unique fingerprints. Hold your head high knowing that you have something to contribute to this world. What you have to offer is valuable, necessary, and needed. Let us look at how we can build up belief in ourselves if it is lacking. Let us live the change!

Building Your Belief Muscle

"I've chosen to move into leadership
so that I can breathe belief into women,
that they can do more, be more,
and have more than they ever thought was possible
& because I was called."
-Jennifer Evans

The way that you view yourself serves as a barometer to determine your personal success. It is great and necessary to surround yourself with those who believe in you. It is equally important, if not more so, that you believe in yourself.

I am often asked, "How did you ignore the negativity and rise above to accomplish your goals?" Part of the answer is this: I am naturally attracted to people who are positive. I avoid negative people like I avoid eating rotten food. Also, I am quick to acknowledge when someone has crossed my path who could be the missing link to something that I need, or I may be the missing link to something that they need. I call these divine connections.

You know it is divine because the hairs on the back of your neck stand up when you begin the conversation. It's a feeling you get, like "I was supposed to meet this person." Those are things we cannot create ourselves. God Almighty places certain individuals along your journey. When you experience these encounters, embrace them, cherish them, and hold on to the connection until your reason for meeting is fulfilled.

The second part of the answer to the question is this: Talk to yourself in a positive way daily, whether you buy a daily motivation book, seek positive quotes, or read the Bible. Whatever you feel are positive words, begin to speak those out loud to yourself every day. Here is some of the positive talk I say aloud:

"I am powerful beyond measure."

"God is my Father, and there is nothing good that HE will withhold from me."

"I am doing my part, and I trust that God will do the rest."

"I will let God lead at ALL times, and I will follow HIM."

Those are just a few of my favorite things I say out loud to myself.

It is so important to hear positive words daily. Speak positivity into your own life and surround yourself with those who speak positivity into your life as well. Take a moment to acknowledge some negative things you may say to yourself. Take this opportunity to replace the negative with positive talk. I started the chart for you to continue.

Positive Talk Chart

Negative	Positive
I cannot do this	I can do ALL things
No one loves me	I am more than enough

Please do not just skip ahead to the next paragraph.
I want you to place the bookmark on this page and
really give it some thought.
Really answer the questions.

I will be right here waiting for you, once you have done so.

This is how we do the work.

This is how we live the change!

I want to share with you something else that I believe is extremely important: I have a very small and close group of friends that I can check myself against. What I mean by that is, I am okay with being wrong about anything. If I am wrong or if I am too hard on someone, these are the individuals who will tell me so. These are people who know me well, truly love me, and are encouraging in my life. However, they will also let me know if I am wrong and if I miss the mark in any situation. Ultimately, I decide how to handle things in my life, but I do trust the input of the advisory board in my life. Having someone like that in your life is so important.

There are times in our lives when we may not feel as confident, especially if we being to embark on a new endeavor. It is so important to have a few faithful people who are supportive and believe in you no matter what. Sometimes it is their belief in me that allows me to push forward until I start to believe in myself. My husband is my greatest supporter and cheerleader. Although he has passed away, I can still feel his encouragement and love wrap around my doubts or fears. I can still hear his words, "Honey, you can do anything." Those are the words that carry me through most days.

Believing in yourself is something that you must exercise. There will always be things in life that will come to cause doubt and fear. You have to choose to exercise your belief until it is a strong muscle. You have to make a conscious decision to exercise your belief muscle daily so it can help you weather the storms of doubt and fear.

As with anything new, you have to practice until you become great. Even those who have accomplished a level of success continue some type of regimen or daily ritual to ensure success.

I've already discussed a few steps you can take to build your own Believe in Yourself routines. To recap:

1. Protect your baby, protect your dreams
2. Surround yourself with positive people
3. Establish positive self-talk daily
4. Have an advisory board you can check yourself against

As you begin to build your belief muscle, you may notice your path will begin to cross with individuals who are either interested in what you desire to accomplish, currently work in a profession similar to what you desire to do, or know someone in your field of interest. The things that you think upon, focus on, and believe in will gravitate towards you like a magnet. This is what is called the Law of Attraction.

As with every other muscle in the body, your belief muscle must be exercised often. While exercising your belief muscle daily, you may notice a more upbeat mood, a sense of accomplishment, and more self-love. Feed your belief, and doubt will starve to extinction.

As you begin to attract the positive into your life, positivity and belief in yourself will fuel your passion, which will ultimately lead you to greater success. Will you live the change?

Your Passion, Your Success!

I once heard the expression that if you love what you do, you will never work a day in your life. I spent many years trying to find that path of self-fulfillment in my own career. After spending some time in deep thought while recovering from my first major injury, I came to the conclusion that I am happiest whenever I am in the mode of creation. I then spent the next few years exploring how I could take the things that bring me pure joy and turn those passions into a way to provide income for myself.

Some correlate success with professional and academic accomplishments. I would like for you to consider expanding your barometer of success to include your passions. Much like joy, passion is a necessary ingredient to add to the flavor of your life. Your passions are closely linked to your gifts and talents.

I truly believe that everyone has at least one gift or talent. Your gift or talent is something you are naturally good at and may operate in with minimal effort. Your talent or gift will bring you joy, a sense of accomplishment, and even the feeling that no one else can do this particular thing quite like you.

Your natural gift or talent may also be your greatest area of confidence. This level of confidence will usually bring you pure joy whenever you engage in that particular activity. It could be problem solving, cooking, drawing, building, etc. I want you to dedicate some real thought to what your creative genius may be.

If you are unsure what you are good at, take some time to explore some things you may be interested in, or create a bucket list of things you would love to do if you knew today was your last day on earth. Allow yourself to experience the curiosity, exploration, wonder, and excitement of making such a list with the intent of accomplishment.

Even if you do not use your talents or gifts to create income for yourself, it is a great way to add balance and joy to life. It is important for you to find the fun and enjoyment in life. What is the purpose of accomplishing all of the things you work so hard to achieve if you do not take the time to enjoy them? Remember the chapter on connecting to your joy?

You may have felt this coming, as you have gotten to know me a bit during this process: I want you to make a list of activities, hobbies, and passions that create some of the emotions that I shared above.

Activities/Hobbies	Passions

These are some emotions you may experience while working in your creative genius: happiness, excitement, joy, laughter, fun, love, gratitude, pride, invincibility, and confidence.

Discovering Your Creative Genius

Things you are good at	*Things that come naturally with ease*

- How does completing this activity make you feel?

_____

_____

_____

_____

- Does it put you in a happy frame of mind to think about things that you are passionate about?

_____

_____

_____

_____

- **Bonus Question**: Can you think of a way to take a hobby or passion and turn it into a supplemental or main source of income?

_____

_____

_____

Please do not just skip ahead to the next paragraph.
I want you to place the bookmark on this page and
really give it some thought.
Really answer the questions.

I will be right here waiting for you, once you have done so.

This is how we do the work.

This is how we live the change!

The idea is to release control and become collaborative by discovering your genius. A collaborative approach can allow you to create just about anything, including your environment. Let us take a look at how to do just that: how to take a situation and create the environment you need during an appointed time.

Chapter 8
Creating Your Own Environment

You are not a victim of circumstance;
your circumstance is an opportunity for you to display
your power and create your own environment!

There are times in life when we choose the circumstances and situations we enter into. Then there are times when the situation enters into our lives uninvited. I know personally, there were times I felt like I was jostled or thrown into a situation that I did not choose for myself. Regardless of the circumstances you are in, you have the power to change your environment once it becomes your personal space to manage.

Know that you are not helpless in your situations. You are powerful beyond measure! Believe in yourself and take the time to tap into your power, talents, and gifts. I want to share with you a story of my earliest memory of me doing the exact things I am suggesting that you do.

When I was about 13 years young, I learned the power of creating my own environment. At this age, I was very settled in who I was as a person and had a strong sense of my individual power. During this period of life, my family lived in a three-bedroom apartment. One of the rooms was what I called the junk room. The junk room was located near the rear of the apartment and was rarely used except to place something there for storage or to look for something you could not find anywhere else. There were tons of plastic bags with out-of-season clothes, unused blankets, an old cot, an end table, a small old TV, and tons of other unused items in that room.

One day, my dad got upset with me about something – if you could ask him, he would probably say it was my attitude. As a punishment, Dad sent me to the junk room. He told me that was going to be my room from now on and I better get used to it. He closed the door behind himself and left me in the junk room.

I stood in the middle of the junk room and began to think. At first, I was upset that Dad banished me to the room where things became forgotten or lost. Knowing he was serious about this being my new room, I begin to think, "How can I take this junk room and make it into something I want to come into every day?" I stood there and imagined what I could do with all of the stuff. I sat on one of the plastic bags, and I saw the old cot and mattress hugged against a corner. I thought, "Hmm, I can make that into a bed." My next thought was, "I could go through all of these bags and see what else I can use." I then rolled up my sleeves and went to work.

I pulled everything out of the closet and began to organize the bags by stacking things neatly into the closet to clear out the room. I then let the cot out and placed the folded mattress on top. I found some clean blankets in the bags and made the cot look like a bed. I grabbed a few stuffed animals out of a bag and placed them on top of my new bed for décor. I then placed the old TV on top of the end table and plugged it in. It worked – now I had some entertainment! A few hours went by, and my dad came to the junk room to check on me. I had completely transformed the room. These were his words: "I'll be damned."

He smirked, closing the door behind him as he left the room. I sat there on my newly made bed watching TV. I continued to decorate the old junk room that I turned into my new little oasis.

That was me, at my best, changing my environment. I knew I was stuck in that junk room, but I also knew that I could use anything in that room to my advantage. Dad said it was now my room; that meant everything in that room I could use. By the next day, I had my certificates and nets with teddy bears on the walls, and it was looking like a beautiful room. The bonus was that there was a bathroom next to my new room as well that no one used (except Dad when he got ready for work at night). The junk room turned out to be a blessing. Dad's punishment placed me in a position where I was no longer sharing a room with my messy little sister. I now had my own room and bathroom. Thank you, Dad!

That was the moment I decided I would never accept a situation I was "thrown into." I promised myself that I would always find a way to make any situation work to my advantage.

To this day, I do the exact same thing. I look at a situation and think, "How can I make this work to my advantage? What blessing lies inside of this situation I did not ask to be in?" Most times, I do not get the answer to those questions right away. But in time, all things are revealed, including answers to my questions.

It is a very human reaction to be upset or angry, as this was my initial reaction when I was placed in the junk room. And I allow myself to explore and embrace whatever feelings I have as a result of a situation or circumstance that "lands in my lap." I always remind myself that complaining never brings results, it just makes me feel more upset. I do, however, allow myself a few moments to be one with my feelings. I am able to vent, be upset, cry, or do whatever else I need to do to express my frustrations. Then I say, "Okay, enough of that, now how do I change this to work to my advantage?"

I invite you to use this approach too. It is very important to allow yourself to acknowledge your feelings and navigate through your emotional process. After the initial emotions you may feel in a situation, take a step back to assess, plan, and take action. Oftentimes, most will take the first steps but stop at "take action." Taking action is the most important step in any process. The action step is the key ingredient to success. Knowing what to do is not enough. The true power is when you can apply what you know, taking action steps towards the changes you desire.

You are not a victim of circumstance; your circumstance is an opportunity for you to display your power and create your own environment!

Are there any situations you feel that you were "thrown into"? These are times when life has handed you a situation that you did not choose. This is not a consequence of a decision or a "bad choice." Take a look at situations that knocked on your door, came inside to live, and you had to deal with it.

- How did you feel?

_____

_____

_____

_____

_____

- Did you allow yourself to embrace or acknowledge your feelings?

_____

_____

_____

_____

- Did you get stuck in your feelings, or were you able to move beyond
  the feeling stage?

_____

_____

_____

_____

- Do you see a pattern of how you deal with situations that "land in your lap"?

_____

_____

_____

_____

Please do not just skip ahead to the next paragraph.
I want you to place the bookmark on this page and
really give it some thought.
Really answer the questions.

I will be right here waiting for you, once you have done so.

This is how we do the work.

This is how we live the change!

I would like to challenge you on something. I strongly believe that the environment we live in daily affects our mood. I want you to take a look around your living space and look for an area that you can make less cluttered, more inviting, and a calming place to rest in. Think of this exercise as a fun mini makeover.

You can choose a closet, your bedroom, bathroom, spare junk

room, or any place in your home. I want you to begin to declutter your chosen space. There is something about clearing clutter that frees your mind. It brings clarity and allows your thoughts to flow more freely.

After you have cleared the clutter, I want you to look at the space and see what things you would like to get rid of, like old furniture, old dust collectors, clothes, etc. Now make a plan for something new or repurpose things in other areas of your home into this space. For example, if you choose the bathroom as your project space, choose a color scheme, paint the wall, and buy some new towels and scented candles. The idea is to give a space a mini makeover and allow it to serve as an inspiration for you.

Do not rush the process; have fun and enjoy creating a new environment for yourself. You can look at magazines, Pinterest, or home design shows for inspiration. You can take one room at a time to gradually transform your personal environment. A mini makeover can be a great compromise to a full renovation and can really boost your mood once completed.

It is a very different feeling when you make a choice about your life versus feeling that life chose for you. Regardless of how a situation comes into your life, I want you to know that you have the power to use change to your advantage and alter the outcome of the situation with the power of choice.

I invite you to take a seat, look around, and see what you can use in your situation to work to your advantage. Turn your junk room into an oasis of happiness. This is an example of how to shift your power.

Chapter 9
Shifting Your Power

You have the power to create the change you desire in your life.

I want you to know that you have the power to create what you desire. You are capable and able to have divine alignment and order in your life. One definition of the word "power" is "the capacity or ability to direct or influence the behavior of others or the course of events." Knowing that you have the ability is one thing; taking that ability and applying it is another.

"Shifting" is a word commonly used in our modern society. I like to use this next description to further elaborate on the subject. When I think of the term "shifting," I often think of driving a vehicle. I have to use the shift to place the vehicle into drive, park, neutral, or accelerated gears, depending on the type of vehicle being driven. You must understand how to use the shift in order for the vehicle to perform in the manner that you expect. You cannot place the vehicle in park and expect for it to be in motion.

The same is true when you are ready to make a shift in your

personal life. If you are ready to implement positive changes into your life, you cannot keep your will or desires in park. You have to take action steps towards change. Developing a plan, executing the plan, and staying consistent are ways to shift your life into motion, while being complacent, having negative thoughts, and giving up are ways to place your life into park. If you understand how to move a motor vehicle, you understand how to move the needle of your life. I stated this once before, and it deserves repeating: you have a brilliant mind and know exactly what to do. It is placing what you know into action that will give you the results that you desire.

I have added a final activity to help motivate and jumpstart your shift of power. If you have completed the activities leading up to this chapter, this should spark a level of excitement and anticipation, so let us begin.

Seven Days to Live the Change

I have always been fascinated with the biblical meaning of numbers. The number seven is the number of completion, so I have chosen seven action steps to help you move into a completed state of one transition to another. The number eight represents new beginnings, so each series of seven lays a foundation to shift into a new beginning. I want you to know that the work of change is an ongoing transition that will evolve as you live your life. Therefore, I am suggesting that in different times and seasons, you may want to revisit the exercises you have completed in this book. This will allow you to see your growth and how your desires may change over time.

As we move towards completing our time together, I want to challenge you to complete this final culminating activity that will bridge all of your self-work together into an action plan. Look over your assignments and pull out the top seven things you want to change over the next seven days. They can be small but impactful changes. The idea is to implement these things and begin to live the change!

Example:

Pending Change	Action
1. Find a new recipe	Cook the meal by the end of the day
2. Restore a relationship	Call up someone you need to have a heartfelt talk with (remembering there is no time like the present)

Live the Change!

Below is a chart to list seven things you would like to implement in the next seven days. You are welcome to use the examples above as a guide to create your own list.

Seven Days to Change Chart

Pending Change	Action
1.	
2.	
3.	
4.	
5.	
6.	
7.	

Once you complete this list, I want you to list one overall goal that you would like to work on immediately (examples: more patience, smiling more each day, working less, spending more time with family and friends).

This total list of eight will put you on track to a new beginning. Continue to work on this list until it becomes second nature to you. Once you master this list of changes, you are free to move on to another Seven Days to Change Chart.

Please note that you may choose to complete a new chart annually or every six months. It is a great way to track your progress, have a system of personal accountability, and witness your personal growth.

This is how we do the work.

This is how we live the change!

Conclusion

When I started this book, I asked your permission to allow me to take this journey along with you. It is my sincere hope that reading these pages has been a journey that will spark positive changes in your life. I hope that you take away a sense of empowerment. I want you to know that you are enough and that you have the power to create the changes you seek in your personal life. How you start the race of life is not as important as how you maintain and finish the race.

If there are things in your life you want to change, I want you to feel empowered to implement those changes. Sometimes we settle because we believe we are unable to achieve the things we truly desire. I want you to give yourself permission to dream and believe that you are capable of taking steps towards the things you truly desire. Live the change!

Oftentimes we know what to do, and it's just a question of making a conscious decision and effort to place what we know into action. Taking action is what helps to usher in a new beginning into our lives. Revisit the pages often where you took notes. Read your goals each day and believe that everything you do is bringing you one step closer to your goals even if you are unable to see it. A major step is a combination of tiny baby steps put together. Live the change!

My desire is for everyone to live an abundant and joyful life. Let us all move beyond accomplishing daily tasks to accomplishing a fulfilling, meaningful, and on-purpose life. Live the change!

I do not have all of the answers, but I am confident that what I have shared is a great stepping-stone. Please use these stepping-stones to embark on your own quest to find answers that are custom made for your life. Questions are always a great way to unlock the answers you are seeking. Become curious, exploring and asking questions of yourself and allowing your exploration to guide you to the answers. Live the change!

Although it is rarely talked about in this day and age, it is important to take personal responsibility for the decisions we make and the actions we do or do not take in our personal lives. It has become popular to blame others for the shortcomings and lack of joy in our lives, but I challenge you to approach life with a sense of personal responsibility. I assure you that this stance is much more empowering. Live the change!

When we blame others, we are saying, "They have all of the power to make my life what they desire it to be." When we take personal responsibility, we are saying, "I may not have made the best decision, but I have the power to turn this around by making better decisions moving forward." Live the change!

My dad who raised me always told me that the things I

experienced were not for myself. My experiences were for me to share with others and to be a servant of inspiration. I now offer those words to you as a gift. Use your experiences to motivate, help, encourage, and inspire another human being. Allow your light to shine brightly, as it may be the only light to bring someone nearby out of darkness.

We are all connected, and if we make it an on-purpose goal to walk in the fullness of joy and personal fulfillment, how much more can we affect and impact the lives of others?

Now go, live an abundant life, be joyful, and pass it on!

This is how we do the work.

This is how we live the change!

~K.C. Lyke

Reference Books

Here are some books that I have personally read and recommend. These are great references if you are looking for resources to help implement change in your life.

Self-Care

Hal Elrod	The Miracle Morning: The Not-So-Obvious Secret Guaranteed To Transform Your Life Before 8AM
Cindy Trimm	Commanding Your Morning: Unleash the Power of God in Your Life

Personal Growth

Tony Robbins	Awaken the Giant Within: How to Take Immediate Control of Your Mental, Emotional, Physical and Financial Destiny!

Laurie Beth Jones	Jesus, Life Coach: Learn From the Best
T.D. Jakes	God's Leading Lady: Out of the Shadows and into the Light
T.D Jakes	He-Motions: Even Strong Men Struggle
Anita Carman	Transforming for A Purpose: Fulfilling God's Mission as Daughters of the King

Relationships

Gary Chapman	The Five Love Languages: How to Express Heartfelt Commitment to Your Mate
Stormie Omartian	The Power of a Praying Wife
Stormie Omartian	The Power of a Praying Husband
Stormie Omartian	The Power of Prayer to Change Your Marriage

Environment

Marie Kondo	The Life-Changing Magic of Tidying Up: The Japanese Art of Decluttering and Organizing
Niki Anderson & Cristine Bolley	What I Learned from God While Gardening

Inspiration

Mary Kay Ash	Miracles Happen

That Which is Greater

The Bible

Elmer L. Towns   Fasting for Spiritual Breakthrough: A Guide to Nine Biblical Fasts